PHILIPPIANS
PHILEMON

ABINGDON NEW TESTAMENT COMMENTARIES

PHILIPPIANS
PHILEMON

CAROLYN OSIEK

Abingdon Press
Nashville

ABINGDON NEW TESTAMENT COMMENTARIES:
PHILIPPIANS, PHILEMON

Copyright © 2000 by Abingdon Press

This book is printed on recycled, acid-free, elemental-chlorine–free paper.

Library of Congress Cataloging-in-Publication Data

Osiek, Carolyn.
    Philippians, Philemon / Carolyn Osiek.
        p.   cm.—(Abingdon New Testament commentaries)
    Includes bibliographical references and index.
    ISBN 0-687-05822-8 (alk. paper)
        1.   Bible.   N.T.   Philippians—Commentaries.   2.   Bible.   N.T.   Philemon—Commentaries.
    I. Title.   II. Series.

    BS2705.3.O75   2000
    227'.607 21—dc21   99-040978

Scripture quotations, unless otherwise indicated, are from the New Revised Standard Version Bible, copyright © 1989, by the Division of Christian Education of the National Council of the Churches of Christ in the United States of America.

Scripture quotations noted AT are the author's translation.

Scripture quotations noted NIV are taken from the *Holy Bible: New International Version.* Copyright © 1973, 1978, 1984 by the International Bible Society. Used by permission of Zondervan Bible Publishers.

Scripture quotations noted RSV are from the Revised Standard Version of the Bible, copyright 1946, 1952, 1971 by the Division of Christian Education of the National Council of Churches of Christ in the USA. Used by permission.

00 01 02 03 04 05 06 07 08 09—10 9 8 7 6 5 4 3 2 1

MANUFACTURED IN THE UNITED STATES OF AMERICA

To all those who have no choice but to take the form of a slave because of poverty, discrimination, and corruption—that they too one day may be raised up.

CONTENTS

FOREWORD

The *Abingdon New Testament Commentaries* series provides compact, critical commentaries on the writings of the New Testament. These commentaries are written with special attention to the needs and interests of theological students, but they will also be useful for students in upper-level college or university settings, as well as for pastors and other church leaders. In addition to providing basic information about the New Testament texts and insights into their meanings, these commentaries are intended to exemplify the tasks and procedures of careful, critical biblical exegesis.

The authors who have contributed to this series come from a wide range of ecclesiastical affiliations and confessional stances. All are seasoned, respected scholars and experienced classroom teachers. They take full account of the most important current scholarship and secondary literature, but do not attempt to summarize that literature or engage in technical academic debate. Their fundamental concern is to analyze the literary, socio-historical, theological, and ethical dimensions of the biblical texts themselves. Although all of the commentaries in this series have been written on the basis of the Greek texts, the authors do not presuppose any knowledge of the biblical languages on the part of the reader. When some awareness of the grammatical, syntactical, or philological issue is necessary for an adequate understanding of a particular text, they explain the matter clearly and concisely.

The introduction of each volume ordinarily includes subdivisions dealing with the *key issues* addressed and/or raised by the New Testament writing under consideration; its *literary genre, structure, and character;* its *occasion and situational context,* including its wider social, historical, and religious contexts; and its *theological and ethnical significance* within these several contexts.

In each volume, the *commentary* is organized according to literary units rather than verse by verse. Generally, each of these units is the subject of three types of analysis. First, the *literary analysis* attends to the unit's genre, most important stylistic features, and overall structure. Second, the *exegetical analysis* considers the aim and leading ideas of the unit, deals with any especially important textual variants, and discusses the meanings of important words, phrases, and images. It also takes note of the particular historical and social situations of the writer and original readers, and of the wider cultural and religious contexts of the book as a whole. Finally, the *theological and ethical analysis* discusses the theological and ethical matters with which the unit deals or to which it points, focusing on the theological and ethical significance of the text within its original setting.

Each volume also includes a *select bibliography,* thereby providing guidance to other major commentaries and important scholarly works, and a brief *subject index.* The New Revised Standard Version of the Bible is the principal translation of reference for the series, but the authors draw on all of the major modern English versions, and when necessary provide their own original translations of difficult terms or phrases.

The fundamental aim of this series will have been attained if readers are assisted, not only to understand more about the origins, character, and meaning of the New Testament writings, but also to enter into their own informed and critical engagement with the texts themselves.

Victor Paul Furnish
General Editor

PREFACE

It is my hope that this volume will stimulate interest in new directions in Pauline studies that are based on new knowledge about the social dimensions of the life of the early Christians and the differences in social perceptions and structures between them and their later interpreters. This is especially true with regard to the part played by social subordinates like women and slaves in the household and thus in the church. We are just beginning to understand how these complex social structures worked and what new pressures were placed on them by Jewish and Christian beliefs.

My thanks go to Victor Furnish, general editor of this series, for the invitation to participate in it, and to my immediate editor, D. Moody Smith, for his patient encouragement along the way. Special thanks are due to the Catholic Theological Union at Chicago for sabbatical time and to the Association of Theological Schools for a Lilly Theological Research Grant during the summer and fall of 1998.

Carolyn Osiek

LIST OF ABBREVIATIONS

1 Clem.	*First Clement*
ABD	*Anchor Bible Dictionary*
AGJU	Arbeiten zur Geschichte des antiken Judentums und des Urchristentums
Ant.	Josephus, *The Antiquities of the Jews*
CBQ	*Catholic Biblical Quarterly*
ConBNT	Coniectanea biblica, New Testament
Ep. Diog.	*Epistle to Diognetus*
HTR	*Harvard Theological Review*
Ign. *Eph.*	Ignatius, *Letter to the Ephesians*
Ign. *Magn.*	Ignatius, *Letter to the Magnesians*
Ign. *Pol.*	Ignatius, *Letter to Polycarp*
Ign. *Rom.*	Ignatius, *Letter to the Romans*
Ign. *Smyrn.*	Ignatius, *Letter to the Smyrnaeans*
JSNT	*Journal for the Study of the New Testament*
JSNTSup	Journal for the Study of the New Testament—Supplement Series
JSOT	*Journal for the Study of the Old Testament*
JTC	*Journal for Theology and the Church*
LXX	Septuagint
NCB	New Century Bible
NIBC	New International Biblical Commentary
NICNT	New International Commentary on the New Testament
NIGNT	New International Greek Testament Commentary

NIV	New International Version
NovT	*Novum Testamentum*
NovTSup	Novum Testamentum, Supplements
NPNF	Nicene and Post-Nicene Fathers
NRSV	New Revised Standard Version
NTS	*New Testament Studies*
Pol. *Phil.*	Polycarp, *Letter to the Philippians*
RSV	Revised Standard Version
SNTSMS	Society for New Testament Studies Monograph Series
WBC	Word Biblical Commentary
ZNW	*Zeitshrift für die neutestamentliche Wissenschaft*

INTRODUCTION: PHILIPPIANS

Philippians is one of Paul's most personal letters, one in which his character and even, one could say, his personality emerges to a certain extent through the rhetorical strategies and arguments by which he crafts his writing. His genuine affection for this community that had been so supportive of him in the past contrasts rather clearly with the sharp directness of Galatians, the fretful worry of 1 Corinthians, or the studied seriousness of Romans. Throughout the letter, Paul's concern for unity and communion comes to the surface in the face of forces both external and internal that threaten the cohesion of the Philippian community. Those forces of dissension, of course, were closely connected to Paul's perception of his own mission and his preaching of the gospel, so that what threatened them threatened him. He also finds himself in a very grave situation and does not know what the resolution will be.

Though we cannot be sure of what exactly the threat consisted, we do know that somehow it involved some of Paul's deepest convictions about how to live a life according to the gospel. In order to counteract it, he draws on the examples of Christ and fellow apostles, and the rhetorical convention of proposing himself as model. Above all the concerns, however, floats the theme of joy. In the letter to the Galatians, in which freedom from law observance is stressed, Paul uses the symbol of the cross more than in any other of his letters. Here in Philippians, the imprisoned Paul, who does not know for sure the final outcome of his confinement, stresses again and again his own joy and that which should characterize his readers.

LITERARY INTEGRITY AND STRUCTURE

Since the early nineteenth century, the literary integrity of Philippians has been questioned by means of the dominant method of redaction criticism, especially because of several abrupt transitions within the letter. The most noticeable is between 3:1a and 3:1b or 3:1 and 3:2, where Paul seems to conclude his thoughts, then suddenly changes the subject with an aggressive attack on the "dogs" who mutilate the flesh. Another apparent conclusion occurs in 4:9, after which Paul launches into a note of thanks for a gift received from the letter's readers (4:10-19 or 20). Commentators notice that it is quite unusual for ancient authors to place such thanks at the end rather than at the beginning of a letter. Moreover, why would Paul wait so long to send thanks for a gift brought from them by Epaphroditus (4:18), delaying until after Epaphroditus had recovered from a serious illness (2:26-27)? At both 3:1 and 4:8, Paul begins what sound like concluding remarks with *to loipon,* often translated "finally." Adding fuel to theories of composite structure is the remark of Polycarp of Smyrna writing to the Christians of Philippi sometime between 110 and 165 CE that Paul wrote "letters" to them (*epistolas,* Pol. *Phil.* 3.2) after he had left them. The various parts of the one surviving letter would be those letters.

Though partition theories have by no means all agreed, the most common proposal is as follows. The first letter (Letter A) would consist of 4:10-20, a short note of thanks for a monetary gift sent with Epaphroditus. There is no direct mention of imprisonment in this section, unless the oblique references to abundance and want in verses 11-12 are indicative of this situation. Letter B is then a composite of several sections, written during Paul's imprisonment on the occasion of his learning of serious dissension in the community: 1:1–3:1a; 4:2-9, 21-23. Finally, Letter C, consisting of 3:1b–4:1, is a spirited defense of Paul's qualifications as a member of Israel and an apostle of Christ in the face of attacks on his law-free gospel. (Arguments on both sides are thoroughly examined by many, including Reed 1997, and a very complete summary of the debate is provided at 125-52 of his book. Garland 1985, 155 lists the major variants on the composition of the three letters.)

Similar arguments about composite authorship have long been set forth in the case of 2 Corinthians, especially around 6:14–7:1, after which 7:2 seems to take up perfectly the topic of 6:13, and chapters 8 and 9 which seem to address an entirely different situation than the rest of the letter, that of the collection for Jerusalem. Such theories posit that as communities began to collect and exchange Pauline letters, for the sake of convenience or efficiency secretaries began to recopy all the letters addressed to one particular place in a continuous or harmonized whole rather than as separate letters, omitting the introductions and conclusions that were thought unnecessary to preserve.

There are of course some problems with these kinds of theories. Such Christian scribes are made out to be either ignorant or careless in the way they roughly juxtapose disparate texts, both situations unlikely in view of the reverence with which Paul's letters seem to have been treated by his communities after his death. The intricacy of the composition of Letter B of Philippians cut into three different pieces is also an unlikely scribal act.

For every argument favoring composite authorship, there is a counterargument favoring the literary integrity of the letter. Modern composite theories presume an intellectual consistency acceptable to a modern literary critic in the writing of an ancient author, but consistency and continuity are cultural values that differ widely. Abrupt transitions in other ancient letters have been identified upon closer look, so that those of Paul would not need to be so unusual. Paul delays the discussion of money in 1 Corinthians until the final chapter, so that the expression of thanks at 4:10-20 is not completely anomalous. The expression *to loipon* at 3:1 and 4:8 can mean not only "finally" but "in summary" of the particular point being made. Polycarp's reference to more than one letter written by Paul to Philippi could be a general rhetorical statement about Paul, always known as a letter writer. Again, there are undoubtedly letters written by Paul that have not survived; it is quite possible that he wrote one or more others to Philippi even after the surviving one, that Polycarp knew, but that were later lost (see 1 Cor 5:9; Col 4:16).

Nearly every commentator sees a parallel between the example of Christ's humility in 2:6-11 and the example of Paul's loss in 3:4-16, with possibly a third example, that of Timothy and Epaphroditus (2:19-30), sandwiched between. Moreover, there are striking verbal parallels between 2:6-11 and 3:20-21. The theory of composite authorship must posit that an editor sufficiently clever to set up these parallels was sufficiently inept to create rough transitions and to cut and paste Letter B in a most awkward way.

Since the middle of this century, there has been a slow increase in numbers of scholars returning to the older assumption of the literary integrity of Philippians, though there is by no means a consensus on the subject. The results of the newer rhetorical criticism have leaned steadily in the direction of the unity of the letter, as exemplified in the seminal study of Watson 1988, who demonstrates that Philippians is a perfectly cohesive whole. The abrupt transitions are explicable from rhetorical theory; for example, 2:19-30 is a "digression" generally related to the topic, after which the author employs startling language to signal a return to the main argument at 3:1-2.

Rhetorical criticism, basing its analysis on ancient canons of rhetoric from Aristotle to Quintilian and Libanius, presumes that since letters such as Paul's were meant to be read aloud to a group, they will follow the rhetorical structures and patterns set out by the great rhetoricians and taught in the rhetorical schools of the day. Unfortunately, we cannot be sure that this is the case for someone of Paul's background or for the particular situations behind his letters. Nor can we even be sure how ancient rhetorical theory was adapted to the letter form. We simply do not know enough about how and when rhetorical rules were applied in nonelite, nonpublic situations or in literature. In recent years, many have analyzed Philippians and other Pauline letters through what we know today about the structures of ancient rhetoric, but no two analyses agree completely. This means at least one of two things: either we do not yet know enough about ancient rhetoric to make its structure perfectly clear to us, or Paul and other ancient writers did not follow it as slavishly as we would like to hope they did, or both. Nevertheless, as rhetorical critics are wont to claim, with a bit more refinement, their method may indeed provide a way out of the impasse with regard to the integrity of the letter.

While proponents of the multiple composition of Philippians may still have some valid points, it is not terribly helpful to study a letter that has been revered and pondered as a whole for twenty centuries as if it were three pieces arbitrarily put together. This commentary therefore will proceed on the assumption of the unity and literary integrity of Philippians.

Several easily identifiable parts of the usual Pauline letter, itself an adaptation of the usual hellenistic letter, are evident at first glance. The *address* or *prescript* (1:1-2) names sender and recipients and adds a brief blessing. The *thanksgiving* (vv. 3-11) adapts the usual short wish for health, prosperity, and the blessing of the gods. A typical thanksgiving section in an ordinary hellenistic letter might say something like "I am well, and I pray to the gods that you are also." The Pauline thanksgiving is usually developed into a longer and more elaborate prayer that both establishes contact by means of general theological language and also prepares for what is to come. It has often been noted that the Philippian thanksgiving passage introduces many of the terms and themes that will be significant later in the letter: joy, sharing, loyalty, perseverance to the end, discernment of what is good, and the announcement of Paul's imprisoned situation. This section corresponds for most rhetorical analysts to the *exordium,* the opening part of the rhetorical delivery that introduces the topic and gets the attention of the audience, especially by praising them for their good qualities.

Then in more general classification comes the *body of the letter,* which continues until the *conclusion* or *postscript* at 4:21-23. Here Paul gets down to the business at hand, the reason for writing the letter and the points that he wants to make. Of course there are many possible subdivisions to such a long section. The first natural unit comprises 1:12-26, where Paul gives an account of his own situation and gives observations about his principal concern, how the gospel is being preached. Some rhetorical analysts identify this section as the *narratio,* the statement of facts that provides the background for the argument to be made. Beginning here, various versions of rhetorical analysis differ, sometimes widely.

At 1:27, a new tone is introduced. Paul is no longer giving facts or talking about his own situation. Attention shifts to the Philippians, and the form of address changes from narration to exhortation. Paul's agenda becomes clearer: he writes not just to fill them in on the facts, or to thank them for their gift (4:10-20), but to address what he perceives as a problem in Philippi. This exhortation to unity really continues from 1:27 to 2:18 before there is a break in the subject. For some, 1:27-30 constitutes the *propositio,* or main point. This analysis is very attractive: the point of the letter is then Paul's appeal to the Philippians from prison, in what might be his final communication with them, to lead lives worthy of the gospel to which they have been called.

What follows are backup examples proposed to the Philippians of how they might pattern their lives according to what Paul has taught them. Many rhetorical analysts would call this whole section the *probatio* or *confirmatio,* the supporting argument provided by examples. The first example is that of the humility and detachment of Christ in 2:1-18, a passage that encompasses the famous christological "hymn" between two direct appeals for obedience and unity. This is paralleled in 3:1-21 by the example of Paul who suffered the loss of all in order to gain Christ. The text of 3:17 is an explicit appeal to imitation of Paul's example. Between these two passages is the discussion of the activity and qualifications of Timothy and Epaphroditus at 2:19-30. This brief section can be seen either as a *digressio,* an excursus that is tangentially related to the topic, or as the second of three parts of the *probatio,* since it gives not only information about the two apostles but also extols them as outstanding examples of obedience and devotion to Paul.

The whole argument can then be summed up in a concluding section of the body of the letter, in which the speaker hopes once again to stir up the feelings of the audience to get them committed to the cause being argued. This section is called in the rhetorical structure the *peroratio*. It is quite uncertain whether the whole of 4:1-20 can be considered a *peroratio*. Verses 1-3 may constitute part of the conclusion of the argument, but it is more likely, and this is the position that will be taken in this commentary, that these verses are in fact the summation, the point to which Paul is leading. Here he gets into particulars about the dispute between Euodia and Syntyche that may be the cause of all the trouble in Philippi. Verses 4-10 are on the subject of joy, not unity, and so seem to have little to do with the main argument of the letter. Verses 10-20, as we have already seen, are the rendering of thanks for a gift received and, again, are not on the subject of unity. It is more likely that Paul has finished with his exhortation to unity at 4:3 and now deals with other topics, thus breaking with the canons of rhetorical structure. This is, of course, one of the arguments of those who propose multiple sources for our document. Finally, verses 21-23 are a rather normal conclusion of a Pauline letter. (A very readable treatment of epistolary rhetorical structure can be found in Murphy-O'Connor 1995, 12-113.)

GENRE

At the highest level of classification, it does not take much effort to decide that Paul's letters are not narratives or epics or apocalypses but *letters*. While today we use interchangeably the two terms "letters" and "epistles," a discussion early in this century led by Adolf Deissmann made a definite distinction between the two terms, a letter being an informal exchange between friends, while an epistle is a literary composition in the form of a letter intended as a medium for philosophical or some other kind of theoretical exposition. Certainly the two different genres existed in the ancient Mediterranean world and at later periods too, by whatever nomenclature one chooses to distinguish them. In this sense writers like Seneca wrote epistles, while Cicero and Pliny the Younger wrote more comfortable and informal exchanges, even though all of the above probably intended their writings from the beginning for publication.

Where would Paul fall on this spectrum? That question has been much discussed. Certainly his letters are not systematic exposition, though they contain elements of it, and Romans may come closest to that genre. Nor, on the other hand, are they only intimate exchanges between friends, though some of Paul's letters, notably Philippians, have aspects of that genre. All of his extant letters are semi-public, meant to be read to at least one house-church (Philemon) and usually to a whole network of them. They are a good example of the elusiveness of genre classification, being somewhere else on the spectrum with elements of all of the above. Actually, the classification of different types of letters by ancient epistolary theorists is much more complex. A good treatment is that of Stowers 1986. Only those immediately relevant to Philippians will be discussed here.

Though not technically a genre classification, the issue of the *societas* model must be raised. In 1980, J. Paul Sampley proposed that the model Paul used in his communication in several instances and particularly with the Philippians was that of the Roman contractual arrangement of this name, whereby two or more partners joined together by mutual agreement for a common purpose and in the pursuit of that purpose were legally bound to the sharing of resources. Within the bounds of the contract, they were considered social equals, though they may not have been otherwise; in fact, Sampley cites (17) the example of a slave entering into such a contract with a free man. Apparently no written contract was necessary, the consent of all involved sufficing. The origins of such agreements seem to have been kinship based, dealing with questions of inheritance among blood relatives. The later use of the custom among nonrelatives is probably therefore a type of fictive kinship.

Sampley argued on the basis of three factors that Paul had entered into such a contractual agreement with the Philippian community: first, the business language of formal receipt used in 4:10-20; second, the frequent use of the terminology of *koinōnia,* which Sampley argues is the Greek equivalent of the Latin *societas* (1:7; 2:2; 4:14, 15); third, the use of other terms in the semantic field of this legal use of *koinōnia,* especially *to auto phronein,* "to think the same" (see 2:2) and related expressions with regard to having the right attitude (1:7; 2:5; 3:15, 19; 4:10). If this theory were true, it would suggest that the predominant model for Philippians would be comment on and further development of the contractual agreement.

This proposal has been seriously questioned in more recent years, however, and other models have been suggested in its place. One is the letter of friendship, and here we have a recognized and widely used ancient genre. The exchange of intimate thoughts and feelings between two friends at a distance from each other was seen as delightful exchange heart to heart, soul to soul. Of course, even some of these letters were written with conscious recognition (even hope!) that they would be kept by the recipient and later made available to a wider audience. The epistolary tradition of friendship was originally elitist, envisioned as possible only between elite educated males of equal social status. While the exclusively male aspect remained, the language of friendship in Roman imperial times expanded into the realm of patronage, so that the terminology was also used in settings of social inequality, in which persons of unequal status bound themselves together, not for the delight of friendship, but for the benefit of each in terms of access to social power and honor. In this context, however, the old connotations of mutual exchange of intimate thoughts and feelings were considerably adulterated.

Though the idea had been previously suggested, the most thorough presentation of Philippians as a letter of friendship is that of L. Michael White 1990. He carefully examines the terminology of the letter and the themes that Paul raises, and concludes that some of the very terminology highlighted by Sampley as contractual is rather the language of friendly exchange, *koinōnia* and *to auto phronein,* among others. He argues that many of the typical expressions of friendship characterize the letter, even though the most basic expression for friendship itself, *philia,* is absent. There are appealing aspects of White's portrayal of this communication of friendship between Paul and the Philippians, for example, that Euodia and Syntyche (4:2) are asked not only to settle their differences but to become friends.

While some have endorsed the basic framework of the terminology of friendship for Philippians, they nevertheless have raised questions about whether this classification by literary genre is adequate. John Fitzgerald (1996), for example, protests that calling Philippians a letter of friendship does not do full justice because it neglects other features that also need attention. Cynthia Kittredge (1996, 132) calls attention to Paul's appeals to obedience in 2:8, 12 as an element with which friendship theory cannot reckon. One might add that the *societas* model would find it equally difficult. Moreover, neither proponents of *societas* nor of friendship have been able to provide parallel examples of one person entering into such relationship with a *group* of people on the other side, as is the case with Paul and one of his communities. Undoubtedly the letter abounds with the terminology of friendship, but classification of it as a letter of friendship does not completely fit, nor does it exhaust the possibilities.

More recently, another model has been suggested by Ben Witherington 1994; that of the "family letter," not a genre recognized by ancient epistolary theorists, but a type of which many examples have been preserved, especially siblings or spouses writing to each other to give news and assurance of continuing affection. The use of parental imagery and the appeal for obedience fit this type, and Paul often refers to himself as father voicing concern and responsibility for his children (e.g., Phil 2:15, 22). Witherington also cites the invitations to imitation as indicative of familial correspondence, but that is not substantiated.

There are other recognizable types discussed and illustrated by Stowers that seem reflected in Paul's letters, even in Philippians: letters of advice and exhortation, of praise and blame, of reproach and consolation. The lack of consensus about the specific genre of Pauline letters is as evident as that about their rhetorical structure.

Occasion and Context

The city of Philippi is located on a plateau of eastern Macedonia, on the western border of Thrace, about ten miles up into pine-forested mountains from its seaport of Neapolis (present day Kavalla) on the north coast of the Aegean Sea. Originally named Krenides ("springs," because of water sources nearby), it was settled by colonizers from the island of Thasos in 360 BCE, the better to have access to the rich gold mines on Mount Pangaion to the west. When the inhabitants appealed to Philip of Macedon against the Thracians, he took control of the city in 356, renamed it for himself, and of course took control of its gold mining operations, too. In the middle of the second century BCE, Roman influence became predominant and the city was a major post on the Via Egnatia, built about 130 to connect the Adriatic coast with Byzantium and the East. From Dyrrachium at the western end of the road, a short trip by boat to Brundisium on the Italian coast enabled the traveler to continue up the Via Appia to Rome.

The city became a Roman military colony after 42 BCE, when the Battle of Philippi, fought on the plains nearby, brought the triumph of Octavian (soon to become Augustus Caesar) and Mark Antony over the assassins of Julius Caesar, Brutus and Cassius. After Octavian's defeat of Mark Antony at Actium in 30 BCE, the city was named Colonia Julia Augusta Philippensis and was given the *ius italicum,* raising it to the same political level as Italian cities. It became a major agricultural and commercial center controlling a vast area of land: the Dados plain to the west, and the passage of the trade route along the Via Egnatia. The presence of large numbers of Roman legionary veterans and their descendants meant a heavy influence of Roman law and Latin language. The vast majority of surviving inscriptions are in Latin, which dominated government life and must have been widely spoken, though Greek was also a current language because of the population of Greeks and Eastern immigrants in the area and the likelihood that they controlled the commercial life of the city.

Because the site is not inhabited today, extensive archaeological excavations have been possible. The large number of votive rock carvings at the acropolis of the city attest to the lively religious faith of devotees of the hellenistic and Roman periods, especially toward the Roman goddess Diana, already syncretized with the Greek Artemis. Unfortunately, most of the buildings now visible were not there in Paul's day, including the magnificent forum of the second century CE. Three later Christian basilica churches and a fifth-century octagonal memorial structure attest to the city as a major Christian center in later years, probably with special devotion to Paul.

If Paul came west into Macedonia in the way depicted by Acts 16:6–17:15, he came by sea from the island of Samothrace by way of Philippi's seaport of Neapolis. It is therefore often stated that Philippi was the first "European" city in which Paul evangelized. Geographically, this is true, but probably not conceptually for Paul and his contemporaries. The distinction between Europe and Asia was known, but the boundary was not clear. Modern readers often read in cultural differences that would not have been as pronounced in the first century. "Asia" as it appears in the New Testament is the designation of a Roman province comprising the western third of Asia Minor, or present-day Turkey, a name parallel to that of Macedonia, the province in which Philippi is located.

One of the puzzles of Pauline scholarship is the discrepancy between stories in Acts about Paul's activities and acquaintances in a particular locale, and the situations and personages reflected in his letters to communities in that same locale. Philippians is a particular case in point. Acts 16:13 presumes a Jewish community. The only supporting archaeological evidence is a late-third-century CE tombstone with mention of a synagogue (Bakirtzis and Koester 1998, 27-35). Acts 16:12-40 presents several lively stories placed in Philippi. The stories of the exorcism of a slave girl with a spirit of divination and the miraculous jailbreak from the resulting imprisonment are framed by two conversion stories, that of Lydia and her household and that of the jailer and his household. The arrest and brief imprisonment narrated by Acts is possibly reflected in Paul's comment elsewhere that he had "suffered and been shamefully mistreated at Philippi" (1 Thess 2:2). Only one local name is given, and the presence of that person dominates the scene: Lydia, the merchant of purple cloth from Thyatira in Asia Minor. Her name is the old designation of the surrounding region in Asia Minor. Since it was often customary to name slaves after their region of provenance, Lydia is most likely a freedwoman. Estimations of her social status based on knowledge of the textile trade vary from wealthy and prosperous to meager and lowly. Both extremes are possible in the trade. The fact that she has a house of her own with dependents, however, suggests at least a relative level of prosperity.

Lydia is the first person in Philippi of whom it is said that "the Lord opened her heart" to receive the word of Paul and Silas, and she is the provider of hospitality for them and the first gathering of those who wish to hear them preach (Acts 16:14-15). Once they have been officially released from detention, they cannot leave the city without again visiting Lydia and those with her (v. 40).

According to Acts, Lydia is the anchoring personality for the foundation of the church in Philippi, yet she is never mentioned in Paul's letter to this church. Even if one wants to argue that she is a traveling merchant who has since moved on and Paul knows that when writing, one would think that he would invoke her memory with the community to recall its foundational identity, much as later Ignatius of Antioch would invoke the memory of Peter and Paul when writing to the Roman church (Ign. *Rom.* 4.3). Yet there is total silence from Paul about Lydia. This kind of noncorrelation is one of many reasons that have led modern scholars to doubt the historical reliability of Acts. But that is a question that cannot detain us here. Other suggested solutions consolidate Lydia to Euodia or Syntyche under a different name. It is simply good to be aware when reading Philippians that there is another side to the story, and the two sides do not fit very well together. However, there is one factor from the two versions that does correlate: the importance of women's leadership in the church at Philippi. Whether it is Lydia according to Acts or Euodia and Syntyche according to Philippians, women are key players in the development of the church there.

The questions of the place and date of writing are very closely linked. One thing is clear about the situation: Paul is imprisoned (1:12-14) and the outcome is not certain (1:19-26; 2:17). But imprisoned where and when? The traditional answer to that question has been Rome at the end of his life. Acts speaks of a two-year house arrest in Rome consequent upon his appeal to Caesar. The references to the *praitōrion* (1:13) and to the household of Caesar (4:22) are most obviously explicable there. The Latin *praetorium,* from which the Greek is a loanword, was originally the office of the commander of a military camp. In Rome it meant the headquarters of the praetorian guard, the elite troops in the imperial service. "Caesar's household," the *oikia Kaisaros,* was the name for the vast network of imperial bureaucracy that was the backbone of Roman administration throughout the empire. The preservation of the terminology of household management reflected the ideology of the empire as one great household with one great patriarchal ruler. The use of the term would also be most evident in Rome, center of imperial administration.

None of these terms speaks decisively for Rome, however. The Roman imprisonment was not the only one for Paul. *Praetorium* was also the term given to the residence of the governor of an imperial province, and the imperial civil service extended wherever there was significant Roman influence. The major obstacle to a Roman provenance is the great distance between Rome and Philippi and the number of visits and letters back and forth that seem to have transpired in a relatively short time leading up to the writing of the letter. The distance between Rome and Philippi is about eight hundred miles and it would have taken probably a month to make the trip. Moreover, in Rom 15:23-24, writing from Corinth, Paul speaks of being finished, of having "no further place" in "these regions," which must be understood as Greece and the East. Instead, he now looks forward to visiting Rome and Spain. On the contrary, he speaks in Phil 1:26 and 2:24 of his intention and hope to return to Philippi.

About the year 1800, an alternative site for Paul's detainment was offered: Caesarea Maritima on the Palestinian coast, where according to Acts, Paul was detained for two years while awaiting trial after his appeal to Caesar. Paul could be under arrest there, thinking that he would stop in Philippi on his way to Rome along the Via Egnatia. Caesarea has the advantage of an explicit reference to the *praetorium,* not of the Roman governor, but of

Herod (Acts 23:35), a clue that the meaning of the word was not closely confined by this time. As residence of the governor of an imperial province, Caesarea would certainly have many members of Caesar's "household." But objections to a Caesarea imprisonment as occasion for the letter are not lacking. Again, distance is a factor. Caesarea is even farther from Rome than Philippi— about twelve hundred miles—and the journey from Rome to Caesarea may have taken as much as two months. If the letter was written from Caesarea, then it still comes late in Paul's career, within the last few years of his life, perhaps as late as the late 50s or early 60s.

A third possible site for the writing of Philippians was suggested early in this century. There are several indirect references to great troubles in Asia or more specifically in Ephesus. In 1 Cor 15:32, Paul refers to having "fought with wild animals at Ephesus," surely not a literal but a figurative allusion to great difficulties. In 2 Cor 1:8-10, he refers obliquely to "the affliction we experienced in Asia" (of which Ephesus was the principal city), where "we were so utterly, unbearably crushed that we despaired of life itself," where it felt that "we had received the sentence of death." It is also remarkable that in Acts' depiction of Paul's final journey as a free man on his way to Jerusalem, he sails past Ephesus heading south, bypassing a city in which he had spent at least two years previously, on the pretext that he is in a hurry to get to Jerusalem by Pentecost (20:16). Then from Miletus he sends for the church leaders of Ephesus, recalling with them the trials he endured there (20:18-19). It does not seem that Paul wants to show his face in Ephesus at that point. Beyond all of this circumstantial evidence, there is the distance factor: Philippi and Ephesus are only about 300 miles apart, and a journey from one to the other probably could have been completed by sea in one week.

There is no definite evidence of an Ephesian imprisonment. A tower near the port is sometimes identified as his place of confinement, but the tradition does not antedate the seventeenth century. Asia was a senatorial province, one of the more politically stable as contrasted to less stable imperial provinces governed by someone directly accountable to the emperor. The conclusion of F. F. Bruce is often repeated, that there is no evidence that the headquarters of the governor of a senatorial province was designated by the name *praetorium*. Thus Asia as a senatorial province would not have a *praetorium* in the original sense. Besides, the evidence suggests that not Ephesus but Pergamon was the administrative capital in which the household of Caesar was more likely to be stationed.

None of these objections is decisive, however. If it were not for Acts, we would have only very general ideas of Paul being imprisoned at all. Use of the word *praetorium* was much broader by the middle of the first century, not limited to a governor's residence or military headquarters, but even used to refer to a large house or palace of royalty or of an important person (Suetonius, *Tiberius* 39; Juvenal 10.161). Proconsular governors of senatorial provinces did not stay in one place, but traveled back and forth to all the major cities and towns of their province to hear judicial cases and deal with necessary business on the spot. Ephesus was the commercial capital of Asia province if not its political capital. Subject to frequent visits by the governor, it must have had some civil service mechanisms in place, the "household of Caesar." If Paul wrote Philippians from an Ephesian imprisonment, then the letter was written several years earlier in his career as an apostle, not toward the end, but perhaps even as early as the mid-50s.

The specific occasion for the letter can only be construed from internal evidence, by which we attempt to reconstruct the story up to the point of writing. Paul's imprisonment while writing is the first fact, whether in Rome or Caesarea toward the end of his life, or, as is more likely, in Ephesus at an earlier stage. The Philippians have been particularly responsive to Paul, more than once sending him gifts of money, and they have done so again most recently by the hands of Epaphroditus (4:15-18). After his last departure from Philippi to deliver the gift to Paul, Epaphroditus fell very ill in the company of Paul, then recovered. Probably Paul had originally intended to have him stay on with him for awhile, but decided instead to send him back to Philippi (2:25-30), either because the community there were so distressed by his illness or because there was little for him to do as long as Paul was not free to work. Paul has also heard, perhaps in a report from Epaphroditus, about the serious rift in the harmony of the community. His concern about this and the opportunity of sending a letter with the returning Epaphroditus provide the immediate occasion for the letter.

THEOLOGICAL AND ETHICAL SIGNIFICANCE

The wider importance of the letter can be seen under four points. First, Philippians raises the question of the relationship of behavior to identity. To whom do the readers belong, and what is the appropriate response to acknowledgment of that identity? Imagery of citizenship is introduced at 1:27 and 3:20, so that Christians are depicted as residents in an alien land. Their own heavenly citizenship requires of them certain distinctive behaviors, just as would be expected for members of a minority cultural group who want to preserve their own heritage.

Second, Paul uses here as elsewhere the imitation theme for formation to Christian life (3:17). He proposes himself and others like him as examples of how to conduct oneself. In doing what seems to modern readers to be a horrendous broach of humility, Paul is simply following the way of the philosophical schools and their pattern of apprenticeship. Nevertheless, it is a vivid reminder that discipleship is learned through observation, imitation, and interaction, and therefore that community has everything to do with gospel living.

Third, the role of *joy* in this letter is remarkable. One could call Philippians the gospel of joy at the heart of suffering. While Paul is imprisoned with an uncertain outcome, while he is burdened with his concern not only for problems in Philippi but in many other churches as well, he can reflect on the sufferings of Christ and on his own, but the sense of joy shines through. His prayer for them is with joy (1:4). He rejoices that Christ is preached at all, even from bad motives (1:18). His survival in this ordeal will give them joy (1:25), while their harmony would give him joy

(2:2). Even if he is to be "poured out as a libation," both he and they should rejoice (2:17-18). They will rejoice to see Epaphroditus back with them once again (2:28-29). He bids them to rejoice in the Lord (3:1; 4:4). They are his "joy and crown" (4:1), whose continued care for him brings him joy (4:10). The presence of joy is pervasive, more noticeably than in any other Pauline letter.

Fourth, the christological poem, the so-called "Philippian hymn" of 2:6-11, is one of the most important pieces of very early reflection on the role and destiny of Christ. As we shall see in the commentary, its interpretation is not without problems, but it stands as proof that very sophisticated christological development was happening within the first Christian generation.

Philippians is a jewel of the Pauline corpus. It reveals Paul at his best and provides us with an exquisite glimpse of Christian life in the first generation of its existence in the Eastern Mediterranean world.

COMMENTARY: PHILIPPIANS

ADDRESS (1:1-2)

The address or prescript is in recognizable form: sender to recipient, greetings. The greetings for Paul are the occasion for a brief blessing or wish not just for material but also spiritual prosperity. (For discussion of the structure of the letter through the categories of ancient rhetoric, see the introduction.)

◊ ◊ ◊ ◊

Paul begins the letter with a greeting from both himself and Timothy, who is with him and known to the Philippian community. His letters often contain another name in the prescript besides Paul's: compare the opening lines of 1 and 2 Corinthians, Colossians, 1 and 2 Thessalonians, and Philemon. In every case except 1 Corinthians, Timothy's name appears, either alone or with another. Timothy was a major and highly esteemed collaborator and assistant of Paul, whom Paul hopes later to send on a brief scouting mission to Philippi, to report back to him (2:19-23). Acts is unclear whether he was part of Paul's first mission to Philippi: 16:3-4 suggests that he was, but in the narratives set in Philippi, his name does not appear alongside those of Paul and Silas. It is also typical of Paul's letters that even though he names a companion or two in the prescript, within a few verses he speaks in the first-person singular, as here in verse 3.

Paul continues in the prescript by calling himself and Timothy *douloi*, "servants" (NRSV), really "slaves," of Christ Jesus. The term "servants" in English carries a somewhat more dignified connotation, but there are other terms for steward or manager in

Greek that Paul could have used to convey that connotation. Instead, he chose the common word for slave—which is not necessarily an expression of humility or debasement. Slavery was a complex and multilayered institution in the ancient Greco-Roman world, by no means to be compared to American colonial slavery except in the common basic injustice of conceiving of human beings as property to be exploited.

In the Greco-Roman world, prisoners of war and condemned criminals in galleys, mines, and public work had a terrible lot, but at the other end of the spectrum, slaves were also trusted and sometimes powerful managers of estates, businesses, and government offices. A slave's status did not derive from the legal condition of slavery, but from the status of his or her owner, the slave's own position, and its importance. Thus for Paul to call himself and Timothy "slaves of Christ Jesus" was to associate themselves closely with the highest-status person available in the social structure of the Christian community. It is a position that demands respect. He will later use the related verb, "to serve" *(douleuein)* for his and Timothy's ministry in 2:22.

Paul next addresses his letter to "all the saints in Christ Jesus who are in Philippi, with the bishops and deacons." Unique to the prescript of this letter is the addition to the community of those two titles of leadership. "Bishops and deacons" are not very felicitous translations for the terms *episkopoi* and *diakonoi* at this very early point in church history, and the NRSV footnotes the preferred alternative, "overseers and helpers." Modern connotations of the words "bishop" and "deacon" are considerably more institutional than anything that existed in the church of the mid-first century. An *episkopos* was an overseer or inspector in various Greco-Roman situations from at least classical times (some examples in Lightfoot 1868, 95-96). The word is also common in the LXX with the same meaning. Elsewhere in the New Testament, the term *presbyteros,* "presbyter" or "elder," seems to be synonymous, for example, the *presbyteroi* of Ephesus in Acts 20:17 are called *episkopoi* by Paul in 20:28. They are a collegial group in the leadership position in a network of house-churches, perhaps the actual heads of those households.

The term *diakonos* occurs many times in the New Testament in slightly different contexts. Paul often calls himself and his coworkers *diakonoi* of God or of Jesus (1 Cor 3:5; 2 Cor 3:6; 6:4; 11:23). In these passages the word probably connotes official representation or agency of an important person, not unlike the title of "slave" as explained above. Only in Rom 16:1; 1 Tim 3:8; and here does the title seem to take on the connotations of some kind of official function in the church, but we do not know what the office entailed. Even the detailed description in 1 Tim 3:8-13, including both men and women, says nothing about what they are actually supposed to do, only about requisite qualities of character.

This verse is one of the earliest indications that Christians have already begun adapting secular leadership terms to life in the church. Other Pauline churches may have used these terms contemporaneously, but if so, it is puzzling that only here does Paul acknowledge persons with these titles. It is more likely that the Roman genius for order and organization has expressed itself earlier in the Roman colony of Philippi than elsewhere. It is likely that the *episkopoi* are a council formed of the natural leaders of the house-churches in the city. We know that women who were heads of households were also leaders of house-churches from the beginning (Acts 12:12; 16:15, 40; Col 4:15). We also know that there were women *diakonoi,* notably Phoebe of Cenchrae (Rom 16:1; probably also 1 Tim 3:11). Because of this corroborating evidence, it is simple bias to assume that the *episkopoi* and *diakonoi* of Phil 1:1 must be exclusively male. Indeed, Euodia and Syntyche may be among either group.

◊ ◊ ◊ ◊

Paul calls the community "saints" or "holy ones." This is one of his favorite expressions for a community: compare Rom 1:7; 1 Cor 1:2; 2 Cor 1:1; Col 1:2. The way it is contextualized in Rom 1:7 reveals the meaning: they are *"called* to be saints" (emphasis added). It is not their own qualifications or character that make them holy, but their identity as *ekklēsia,* those called by

Christ's initiative to be his holy assembly, just as in the past Israel was called out from the nations by God.

The blessing that concludes the prescript is simple and typically Pauline. "Grace" *(charis)* is a word that originally meant "gracefulness" or "favor," but for Paul has taken on the meaning of the special kind of favor that comes only from God. The wish of peace is the *shalom* that is still the ordinary greeting in spoken Hebrew. But here, grace and peace are those that only God and Jesus can give. The blessing is Paul's more common twofold "binitarian" form rather than trinitarian. While Paul has a very active theology of the Holy Spirit and sometimes includes the Spirit in blessings, the triadic formula is not yet in common use. Triadic patterns do appear outside of blessing formulas in the letters, for example, 1 Cor 12:4-6.

THANKSGIVING (1:3-11)

Verses 3-11 constitute the next recognized section of a Pauline letter, expanded from the simple wish for prosperity and health that is characteristic of the hellenistic letter at this point. The general structure follows the thought line: "I thank God for you because . . ." (here vv. 3-8), "and I pray for you that . . ." (vv. 9-10). This passage in Philippians is the most extended and developed of the thanksgiving sections in the Pauline letters.

◊ ◊ ◊ ◊

Paul gives thanks using the ordinary verb to convey that meaning, *eucharistein*. The noun *eucharistia* has not yet become linked with a ritual meal that Paul refers to as the Lord's Supper (1 Cor 11:20). He is grateful for their *koinōnia*, "sharing" or "partnership," terminology that could be used in business contracts, but that in daily life and especially in Christian usage has a much broader meaning of sharing experience and labor. The idea is repeated in verse 7 using a related noun. Later, he will use the same word to appeal to the recipients to unite in the Spirit (2:1).

Another important term that is introduced is *phronein,* here translated "think" (v. 7). A broader sense of the word could be conveyed by the ideas of having an attitude or an orientation toward something. Later in the appeal to unity at the beginning of chapter 2, this terminology will reappear.

When in verse 8, Paul longs for them with the "compassion" of Christ Jesus, the Greek word so rendered is *splangchna,* literally the inner organs, including heart, lungs, liver, and intestines. Its literal meaning appears in Luke's description of the death of Judas (Acts 1:18). Paul uses the term in its well-established secondary meaning of feelings, especially those of affection and mercy. This meaning reveals the awareness of ancient Mediterranean people that emotions produce a physiological effect felt in just those organs. The language in this verse is typical language of letters of friendship.

The thanksgiving sets the tone for the rest of the letter. It is relaxed, expansive, and charged with positive energy. Most of the major themes to be developed in the letter are already present here: Paul's gratitude and affection for the Philippian community, their sharing in the Gospel, his imprisonment, his wish for their "knowledge and full insight to help you determine what is best" (v. 9). Only his explicit concern for their problems about unity is missing, and could well be subtly included in the "knowledge and full insight" of verse 9. The previous RSV translation was "knowledge and all discernment," which may express more clearly what is at stake here, not insight in general but insight about the things of God, and how to recognize the Spirit at work and commit to following the Spirit's bidding.

The sequence of the second part of the passage is interesting: Paul prays that their love may overflow into knowledge and insight that will make them come out well on the day of Christ Jesus. We would expect knowledge to lead to love, but Paul puts it the other way around. It is their response to the love of Christ for them that will give them the right knowledge. This is the process begun in them by God, about which Paul expresses his confidence in God's fidelity to bring completion to the work already begun (v. 6).

The beauty of this thanksgiving section can be better appreciated by comparing it to others written by Paul: the terse Rom 1:8-10; 1 Cor 1:3-9; and 2 Cor 1:3-7; the more expansive 1 Thess 1:2-10 and Phlm 4-7; and Galatians, where it is completely absent!

PAUL'S SITUATION (1:12-26)

This section begins the body of the letter and introduces the reasons for writing by giving some background to the situation. While much of its expression is intensely personal, it is at the same time composed within recognizable rhetorical patterns: reassurance and encouragement of followers, critique of the unworthy motives of others, philosophical reflection on the burdens of life, and anticipation of release (compare for instance 2 Tim 4:1-8). The section consists of three parts. In verses 12-14, Paul gives his perception of the situation: what seems disastrous is not. In verses 15-18, the motives of others are questioned but the outcome is embraced. In verses 19-26, he reflects on his own dilemma about his future.

◊ ◊ ◊ ◊

Paul begins with an expression, "I want you to know" (*ginōskein de hymas boulomai),* which is a common construction to impart information. He calls the Philippians "brothers" *(adelphoi),* as he ordinarily addresses members of his churches. Two different kinds of observations must be made about Paul's use of this title. First, it connotes equality rather than a superior/inferior relationship as is the case with paternal imagery (2:22; 2 Cor 11:2; 1 Thess 2:11) or sometimes maternal imagery (Gal 4:19), which he uses on occasion. While Paul is quite conscious of his authority in the communities he founded, he nevertheless does not address them as social inferiors—and there were many ways in status-conscious ancient Mediterranean culture to do so.

The second observation is that *adelphoi* is a masculine plural form of address. Besides being heavily status-conscious, Paul's world was decidedly androcentric. Even in public places, the speakers in Acts usually address their audiences as *andres adelphoi,* "males, brothers." This does not mean that Paul intends to exclude the women of the congregation in his address, nor that Luke thinks that there are no women present in the marketplaces where he situates the speeches of Peter, Stephen, or Paul. Though all models of social interaction are stereotypes that cannot deal with the complexity of real social exchange, it can generally be said that in the ancient Mediterranean world, public space was male space, while private domestic space was that of females, at least at certain times of the day. Even though there are women present in house-churches when Paul's letters are to be read, even though there are women present in the agora of a city when Paul preaches in Acts, they are not recognized in speech and so are socially invisible while physically present. In Philippians, the proof of this linguistic convention is that in 4:2, two women who are significant in the community will be addressed by name.

Paul's imprisonment (literally, his "chains," but which need not mean that he is literally chained), undoubtedly seen by the anxious Philippians as a disaster, has in fact been the occasion of free publicity for the cause. It has encouraged those who might have been hesitant, because Paul has become unexpectedly famous right where he is. Thus the reason for his imprisonment, the advancement of the gospel, has become well known in the whole *praetorium,* the governor's residence or the military nerve center or prominent location where he is confined (Matt 27:27; Mark 15:16; John 18:28, 33; 19:9; see Introduction for further discussion of the difficulties involving the term).

Every good defense requires an equally good offense. As with the "dogs" of 3:2, the threat of opponents strengthens the cause. The language in verses 15-18 picks up the accusations of persuasive rhetoric: envy and rivalry, selfish ambition, sharply contrasted with those whose motivation is love. He even accuses them of trying to cause him trouble and suffering in his confinement. Some of them may be imprisoned with him and causing dissension within the prison. Clearly, he has no respect for them. We know nothing else about these alternate Christian preachers except what we can learn from Paul's critique of them. They may have been perfectly well-intentioned missionaries whose strategy or way of operating was in disagreement with that of Paul and his companions. Accusation of false motives and even sometimes moral turpitude by "the others" is a stock part of such defense (cf. 2:21). Ignatius, for example, writes that those who believe differently, the heterodox, neglect widows, orphans, prisoners, and the needy (Ign. *Smyrn.* 6.2). These people of whom Paul is not overly fond were probably not a huge threat. Attacking the outsiders strengthens the boundaries of, and one's position among, the insiders.

One thing that comes through in verses 15-18—as if we did not know it from other sources—is that Paul does not get along with everyone in the churches. But here we see a mellower and more detached side of him than in the fiery defenses of 2 Corinthians. Paul does not try to retaliate against what he experiences probably as the pettiness and jealousy of other Christian missionaries. The language he uses for their conduct, *phthonos, eris* (v. 15), and *eritheias* (v. 17) are typical of literary tracts against factionalism and partisanship, and usually imply the imputing of ill will (Winter 1994, 94-95). The first of these words, especially "envy," carries with it a world of social connotation about resentment at the success of others. It is often associated with sorcery, the evil eye, and other ways of actually causing harm to the one envied. On the other hand, to be envied, as Paul says he is, is a mark of honor that one has been sufficiently successful to bring about this reaction.

Even in the middle of this additional unwelcome difficulty, Paul has the freedom to rejoice that Christ is being preached one way or another. Here perhaps "the gentleman doth protest too much," since in 3:1 he will have very definite and very sharp objection to another way of preaching the gospel, and Galatians is an entire letter written to object to just that. Here at the conclusion of verse 18 is the first echo of the theme of joy introduced at verse 4. It is a theme that will pervade the entire letter.

The expression of joy is the transition from one topic to

another, from verse 18 to verse 19. Paul rejoices that Christ is preached, and will continue to rejoice for another reason: through their prayers he will see a positive outcome to what he now slowly admits is a grim situation. In verses 19-26 Paul reflects on his plight and its implications for the future. The way it is structured is traditional, yet the person Paul, with his own human doubts and faith, also comes through. He begins with an allusion to Job 13:16, an exact quotation of five Greek words from the LXX text that mean "This will turn out for my salvation." One can only wonder whether these words leapt up to him from childhood Bible memorization, or whether he saw some similarity between his predicament and that of Job, who also longs for vindication and is maligned by those who should be supporters (cf. Hays 1989, 21-24).

The rest of verse 19 speaks of the means by which Paul hopes to be saved, not political strategies or the exercise of power—though others may have been working with these means to get him freed—but he concentrates here on the real power behind such efforts. Their prayers of intercession, he believes, can make a real contribution to the cause, joined with the provision of the Spirit of Jesus Christ. The word *epichorēgia*, translated as "help" in the NRSV, should probably rather be understood as provision or "supply," that is, that the Spirit is grammatical object, that which is supplied, rather than grammatical subject who supplies (Fee 1995, 132-33). God gives the Spirit in abundance where needed, as is obvious here.

The theology of the Holy Spirit is under development in Paul's letters. It is the biblical Spirit of God that is now possessed by Jesus and the community. Sometimes in passages like this one, the exact meaning of the word *pneuma* is ambiguous. There is also the human spirit, for which the same word is used, and which according to hellenistic psychology is the human capacity for the infinite. One of the most confusing passages in this regard is 1 Cor 2:10-16, where the same word has several different meanings that can only be known from context. Likewise, 2 Cor 3:17 with its seeming equation of the Lord and the Spirit throws off track any attempt to elucidate a clear theology of the Spirit in Paul.

In English we capitalize the word when referring to the Holy Spirit, otherwise not. Ancient Greek manuscripts did not capitalize special words, so there is no way of knowing for certain whether the *pneuma* spoken of here is the Holy Spirit of God, or the risen and glorified human spirit of Jesus, or both. Paul seems to think of the Holy Spirit as the action of God to create one community through baptism and to bestow spiritual gifts of prophecy, tongues, and other less conspicuous functions for the building up of the community (1 Cor 11:4-13). The Spirit is the power that animates both Jesus and the community, given as gift and pledge of what is promised to us for the future (2 Cor 1:22). Thus here in our passage, it is best to understand that Paul is speaking of the Spirit of God that animates the Risen Jesus and the community as his body. God bestows the gift of this Spirit on Paul in prison, which enables him to have the bold confidence that he has.

Verse 20 is full of the "loaded" language of honor and shame, the key cultural values of the ancient Mediterranean world. Following so soon on the quotation from Job, the concern about being shamed also echoes biblical passages like Pss 25, 34, 35. Maintenance of a public reputation for honorable conduct and the ability to defend oneself and one's family successfully against attack were essential qualities for any free male. Confidence and assertiveness were the characteristics of honorable males, while modesty, shyness, and reticence were the essentials of conduct and appearance for females. For a man to be arrested and detained in the shameful condition of loss of freedom was damaging not only to his sense of self but to his public reputation. That is the situation in which Paul finds himself, and to which he alludes here, but only to assure his readers that honor is coming through shame.

Paul's eager hope is that he "will not be put to shame in any way." There were many ways to be put to shame, but probably the primary one in this expression refers to judicial condemnation. He is probably alluding at the first level to an upcoming judgment or trial, where he believes that he will be vindicated. If the setting is an Ephesian imprisonment in the mid-50s, he was apparently correct in his intuition that he would be vindicated. If the scene occurred later in a Caesarean or Roman imprisonment, it is less likely that his intuition and hope were correct. But Paul also looks beyond his present condition, which can only be construed as public shame, to transcend that shame and transform it into the honor of Christ.

In the midst of this public shame, he speaks "with all boldness" *(en pasē parrēsia)* (v. 21). *Parrēsia* refers to the open, direct, and honest speech ("telling it like it is") that was not permitted to women, slaves, or certainly not to prisoners, but only to free men. It was the special privilege of the freeborn, especially the elite male. Paul virtually ignores his shameful situation, caught up in the honor of Christ that is being won through his bold speech, and that will come through no matter what the outcome for himself. He is enabled to do this through the gift of the Spirit that is supplied by God (v. 19).

In verses 21-24 Paul meditates aloud on the alternative outcomes over which he has no control. He expresses an indifference to life and death that should be related to 4:11-13 where he speaks of himself as *autarkēs,* a concept especially revered by the Stoics as a level of inner freedom that results from reducing outer needs to a minimum. Actually the statement here in chapter 1 is the more radical: Paul says he is indifferent even to life or death— and he is facing the real possibility of death. His attitude here must be seen in light of 3:20-21, the idea that the real home of Christians is elsewhere and the expectation of deliverance comes from elsewhere.

In verse 21, Paul says that continuing to live means union with Christ, while dying is gain because it is the completion of that union. This idea of death as gain must be seen in light of the discussion of gain and loss at 3:7-8 and the philosophical tradition of the noble death of one who dies with dignity for the truth. He is playing with the concepts and reversing them in a particular way that serves the purpose of rhetorical effectiveness but that is also characteristic of his theology. His dilemma of verse 22 about which to prefer, life or death, is a rhetorical one. It is unlikely that Paul thinks he will ultimately have any choice in the matter.

The turning point of Paul's reflection is between verses 23 and 24. His own choice is death in order to be sooner with Christ and

to bring to completion in his own life the process of dying and rising with Christ that he has been presenting as the model of
Christian life. Paul frequently uses the expression "in Christ" as
both personal and communal incorporation through baptism in
the mystery of his death and resurrection even in this life. Here
something different is meant. To be "with Christ" is to have left
this life and to have realized the fulfillment of that earthly incorporation in full union. This is necessarily the preferable option,
consistent with the kind of life he has been leading and the gospel
he has been preaching. Yet he recognizes that his communities
need him. The Philippians have no doubt made it very plain that
they will be bereft if he dies now. His conviction, then, expressed
in verse 25, is not his personal preference but his assurance in
faith of what God will do: bring him through this trial in order to
continue to be of service to those who need him. He plays on the
word "remain" *(menein)* by adding to it a compound of the same
verb *(paramenein)*, which does not have a clearly different meaning. The NRSV "remain and continue" (v. 25) says it as well as
possible in English.

In the long run, Paul sees that *God* must have a preference in
this dilemma, to have Paul continue to live for the sake of the
churches. The expression of this conviction in verses 25-26 is a
statement of boldness or confidence that assures the Philippians
that the forces against him will not win. Rather, they will have
occasion for greater joy and advancement in the gospel through
his survival and return to them. Then they will have reason to
boast in Christ because of Paul.

The expression of boasting *(kauchēma* or *kauchēsis)* is one of
the most misunderstood Pauline concepts when we read it from
the context of contemporary acceptable expressions of pride and
humility. *Kauchēsis,* the act of boasting or taking pride in something, has ancient connotations of pushing one's own honor too
far so as to tempt or challenge even the gods. However, it also has
overtones of the maintenance of public honor by insisting that
one's status be appropriately recognized. It is part of the semantic
field opposite shame (e.g., 2 Cor 10:8). For Paul, this boasting is
usually a positive deed because there is only one reason for which

to boast: not of one's honor or accomplishments, but only of what God has done for us and in us.

Kauchēma, the word used in verse 26, normally means not the act of boasting but the object in which one takes enough pride to boast, though sometimes the two words seem to be used interchangeably. The classic passage for Pauline boasting is 2 Cor 11:16–12:10, where Paul sarcastically refutes his opponents whom he depicts as overdoing the boasting. In retaliation, he will boast of visions and revelations, making himself out to be an important spiritual person—only to end with his humiliation because of the "thorn in the flesh" (see 2 Cor 12:7-10), symbol of the hardships and afflictions endured by Paul for the honor of the gospel.

Verse 26 contains the kind of syntactical jumble that is not unusual in Paul's letters. It reads literally: "So that your reason for boasting *(kauchēma)* might abound in Christ Jesus in me because of my coming *(parousia)* again to you." The NRSV attempts an interpretation that introduces some extra terminology to make the meaning clearer: "so that I may share abundantly in your boasting in Christ Jesus when I come to you again." It is perhaps not Paul's sharing in their glory that is meant, but that he will be the occasion of it when he returns to them. He looks forward, as one now in a bad situation, to a future time when everything will be set right again, and they will be able to glorify God not only because of Christ but also because Paul has been set free and sent back to them. His visit will be a *parousia,* a term usually referring to some kind of official or important visitation, later to become a technical term for the "final coming" of Christ eschatologically. Obviously, at Paul's writing the word has not yet acquired this exclusive meaning, though Paul also uses it in this way (1 Cor 15:23; 1 Thess 2:19; 3:13; 4:15; 5:23).

◊ ◊ ◊ ◊

Without ever using the term "cross," this passage introduces Paul's theology of participation in the death and resurrection of Jesus that is also developed in different ways elsewhere, particularly in Galatians and later in Phil 2 and 3. The starting points are the cultural centrality of gaining honor and avoiding shame, and the historical fact of Jesus' death as a public criminal, as he was condemned to die in one of the most shameful ways ever devised. These two pieces of data clash with resounding force for one who is convinced that Jesus is the Messiah and Son of God. Every New Testament writer who grapples with this dilemma, notably the evangelists, Paul, and the author of Hebrews, has to resolve it in some way.

Paul's resolution is to reverse the usual social expectation—and this is the radical cultural reversal inherent in Pauline and some other forms of Christianity, because the cross of Jesus, outwardly shame, becomes honor in God's vindication of Jesus in the resurrection. Thus what is supposed to be shame is really honor and what is supposed to be honor is really shame; gain is loss and loss is gain. That is why he can rejoice in prison and in the fact that the gospel is being preached, no matter what, even though his own situation is precarious. That is why his heart moves in two different directions when trying to anticipate an outcome. Death is not fearful, nor is continuing to live. Both mean further life with Christ. Death would not mean a peaceful transition from one state to another, from mortal life to some kind of afterlife as in the Greek notion of immortality. Though he does not specify here, he will do so later in chapter 3, that death means the completion of the process of transformation into Christ that is only brought to fulfillment in conformity to his resurrection.

The Philippians, too, are closely connected with Paul in this anticipated transformation. All is for the sake of the advancement of the gospel. This is the point at which he and the Philippians are partners in the cause (vv. 5, 7). So his failure would be theirs by participation, but his success is theirs, too.

Whatever the outcome of Paul's predicament, Christ will be honored, either by his death for the cause of the gospel, or by his deliverance that will enable him to continue to preach and to be a leader for his communities. Paul's statement that no matter what happens Christ wins implies, of course, his own victory with Christ. Besides being a profound expression of human freedom through faith, it is also a clever way of beating the system: no matter how dishonorably you treat me, no matter how much you shame me, the outcome is honor no matter what. This is the attitude of later martyrs and even suicide bombers in the face of official opposition and threat. Nothing more can be done to the one who does not fear death.

APPEAL AND ENCOURAGEMENT (1:27-30)

At verse 27, there is a marked change in the style of the letter, a shift from first-person narrative and indicative mood to the predominance of the second-person plural in the imperative mood, which will continue, except for occasional side statements and the narrative example given at 2:6-11, until 2:18. The chapter division between 1:30 and 2:1 is somewhat artificial. Verses 27-30 can be seen as the central statement of the letter, the real message that Paul wants to get across to the Philippians. It is not unrelated to what has just gone before: the anticipation of another visit of Paul. These verses say how he wants to find them. In Greek, all of verses 27-30 are one sentence, all dependent on one main verb, *politeuesthe*.

◊ ◊ ◊ ◊

Politeuesthe is a second-person plural imperative that is commonly translated "conduct yourselves," "live your life" (NRSV), or the like, which takes the punch out of it. The word really means to live as citizens, to exercise your citizen's rights, to conduct yourself in a manner worthy of citizenship. It is used in a similar way of Paul's life as a Jew in Acts 23:1. Picture Paul here, a Roman citizen (according to Acts), writing to Christians in a city founded as a Roman colony, with extensive Roman influence and a large number of Roman citizens, mostly Latin-speaking, with Greek as a second language. The choice of words in this central statement of the letter is not accidental.

Citizenship in any ancient city was not given automatically to anyone born there, but came through family and social position. Only those persons whose family possessed the right of citizenship, or who had acquired it by official conferral in exchange for some extraordinary service rendered were citizens of any city. Roman citizenship in this period was granted in a variety of ways as a reward for loyalty to Rome, to slaves of Roman citizens manumitted in the correct way, or sometimes at this period by purchase (see Acts 22:28). Roman citizenship carried with it throughout the empire certain privileges, especially for those accused of a crime. See, for example, the trouble caused by Paul's Philippian and Jerusalem arrests when his jailers learn that they have beaten and imprisoned a Roman citizen (Acts 16:37-39; 22:24-29).

At this point, Paul begins in earnest the appeal to unity that will continue through most of the letter. The concern for harmony in the face of civil discord was something of a preoccupation of writers of this period, an indication that, while individualism was not the problem, factions and divisive groupings surely were. The concern surfaces in several Pauline letters, notably to the Corinthians (1:10-17 *passim*). Paul's appeals do not seem to have been totally effective, for later in the century Clement of Rome will write to the Corinthian Christians a well-crafted rhetorical address known as *1 Clement,* urging them to abandon their factions and be unified under traditional leadership. He exhorts his listeners to harmony and union in language reminiscent of civic appeals to concord. Indeed, one of the possible meanings of the verb *politeuomai* that is used here is for a group of citizens to function publicly in harmony (Winter 1994, 102). So Paul draws on the Philippians' experience, identity, and sense of honor as Roman citizens.

That is not all, however. Paul is speaking on two different levels here. Clearly from the beginning of the appeal, he is talking about much more. They are to live as citizens of the gospel of Christ, whether or not Paul is there to guide them. The "gospel" here, of course, does not yet mean a written document, but the whole way of life they learned along with the proclamation of Christ in the preaching of Paul and the instruction of their local teachers. They are to be in one spirit *(pneuma)* and "one mind" (NRSV) or soul *(psychē)*. One way to read this double statement of verse 27 is that it is literary parallelism as in Hebrew poetry, the second term therefore essentially repeating and supporting the first. "Spirit" then would mean corporate feeling of unity. But as Fee (1995) points out, Paul never uses *pneuma* with that meaning. Rather, the one spirit is the Spirit of God who gives all spiritual gifts, in whom all are baptized, and of which all drink (1 Cor 12:4-13). The second term, *psychē,* is used by Paul and others to mean human consciousness and effort or mortal life (Rom 2:9; 13:1; 16:4; 1 Cor 15:45; 1 Thess 5:23).

The passage begins with an appeal to unity, but as it progresses, the sense of dualism and threat deepens. The Philippians are to stand firm and not be intimidated by opponents or by drawbacks and suffering. Their firm endurance in the face of opposition will stand as a sign of contradiction that they are progressing toward salvation, their opponents toward destruction. This is the first mention of opponents, a difficult category in this letter because it seems that the ground under them keeps shifting. The reference is not simply to those other proclaimers of the gospel whom Paul had accused of unworthy motives (1:15-17). The language here is stronger and more like that of 3:1.

While language of citizenship introduces the point in verse 27, through these verses also runs the metaphor of athletic competition. The Philippians are standing firm in one spirit, but "striving side by side" *(synathlountes)* in one soul, as if working together in athletic conditioning to be able to stand up to the test. The athletic situation is competitive enough, but when used metaphorically outside the strictly athletic context, the word carries connotations of hard struggle in great difficulties, as does another athletic term used in verse 30, *agōn,* translated "struggle" in the NRSV. The first, *synathlein,* will also be used to describe Paul's solidarity with the two women at odds in 4:3. Though the distribution of athletic metaphors is wider, terms related to these appear in the New Testament only in 2 Tim 2:5 and Heb 10:32. Here the prefix is significant: *syn-* (with, together). It is not only a struggle in which Paul or they are engaged, but they share the common struggle, just as they are partners or sharers *(synkoinōnoi)* in his grace even in imprisonment (1:7).

These verses especially have led some commentators to conclude that there is some kind of active persecution going on in Philippi, and that that is a major reason why Paul is writing the letter. Others suppose that this is a passing conventional reference to the necessity of suffering in the Christian life, or a projection of his own present experience. Use of terms like "opponents" certainly suggests a hardened we/they attitude, which could also be eschatological, but other than this word, there is a notable lack of eschatological terminology in the passage. The occasion must be sought elsewhere. Any well-constructed rhetoric of solidarity must present a crisis situation in which there is an external threat. We will have further occasion to consider this question at 3:1.

Perhaps what is causing the disunity in the church is precisely the experience of suffering. A full-blown persecution by Roman authorities is hardly necessary. Shunning, public embarrassment, nonrecognition of personal honor and status, discrimination in the patronage system because of their beliefs—these would be sufficient factors to cause a great deal of discomfort on the part of new believers who have heard words about persecution but now experience it for the first time.

Use of the terminology of citizenship here in 1:27 must be seen in relation to 3:20, where the analogy is clearer, and where there will be further comment: our *politeuma,* that is, the home base of our group, is not here but in heaven. Christians are like a group of aliens from another city who live together in this city while not fully belonging to it because they do not have citizenship here. This was an actual situation that was quite common in the Greco-Roman world. These verses use a real situation of many groups of people as a metaphor for Christian identity in the world. First Peter does something similar with its use of the terms *parepidē-mos* and *paroikos* meaning "stranger" and "resident alien" (see 1 Pet 1:1, 17; 2:11). It must not have been easy for Roman citizens of Philippi, citizens from birth or those who had perhaps had to work hard to acquire their citizenship, to hear that in what really mattered, they were not actually citizens of the place where they lived after all. This attitude sets up a certain tension with a theology of responsible ecology or administration of earthly realities.

The shadows deepen as verses 29-30 continue. A new spiritual gift has been granted to them on behalf of Christ. Their first belief and continuing faith is certainly just such a gift, but now they have been given more: the grace also of suffering for him. In this way, the Philippians become partners or participants with Paul in a deeper way. What they have seen and heard of him, they also experience. It is as if Paul is saying "I told you so. You've heard me talk about it. You've received reports of it happening to me. Now it is happening to you."

ENCOURAGEMENT TO UNITY THROUGH HUMILITY (2:1-4)

These verses, which are usually passed over on the way to the hymn that begins in verse 5 or 6, have a definite structure: four "ifs," a chiasm, and two statements of what not to do and what to do by contrast. Verse 1 consists of four "if" clauses, obscured by the NRSV translation that does not repeat them: "*if* then there is any encouragement in Christ," *if* there is "any consolation from love," *if* there is "any sharing in the Spirit," *if* there is "any compassion and sympathy. . . ." Verse 2 consists of a result statement and a chiasm or inclusion structure. Following the four conditional statements of verse 1, verse 2 continues, "then fulfill my joy by" followed by four statements. The first and fourth of these statements say the same thing, as do the second and third. Verses 3-4 contain two statements structured as "not this, but that" "nothing from . . . ambition or conceit, but . . . regard others as better than yourselves . . . not to your own interests, but to the interests of others."

◊ ◊ ◊ ◊

Several expressions in this brief passage deserve special comment. The first two "if" clauses of verse 1 feature two words that are probably synonymous: *paraklēsis* and *paramythion*. They are translated "encouragement" and "consolation" in the NRSV, but both Greek words can mean either English word, whose meanings are really somewhat different, for they could be considered as an antidote for dejection and for grief, respectively. *Paramythion* occurs in early Christian literature through the Apostolic Fathers only here, while its synonym *paramythia* appears only in 1 Cor 14:3. The first term *paraklēsis*, however, is ubiquitous, with both meanings of it stirring up commitment through encouragement or calming fears through consolation. Because the experience behind it is so connected with emotion and feeling, it is often closely related to the work of the Spirit especially in prophecy (e.g., Luke 2:25; Acts 9:31; 13:15; 15:31) as is its cognate *paramythia* with which it appears in 1 Cor 14:3.

The third word in this fourfold construction in verse 1 is *koinōnia*, sharing or partnership, which has already appeared as a significant term in 1:5 as the bond linking Paul to the Philippians. Here it is *koinōnia pneumatos*, sharing in spirit, probably to be understood as sharing or participation in the Holy Spirit. As in 1:27, it would be very unusual for Paul to use this word to mean a general sharing of enthusiasm, since by *pneuma* he usually means the Spirit of God or the human spirit in relationship with that Spirit (as in 1 Cor 2:10-16). Though terminology of prophecy is not present in this passage of Philippians, the use of *paraklēsis* and *paramythion* followed by this expression of life in the Spirit suggests prophecy as a background.

The fourth "if" clause is about compassion and sympathy (*splangchna* and *oiktirmoi*), attitudes closely associated with the nature of God and of Jesus. Paul is beginning to build up his appeal for unity. He will achieve this by pointing to the example of Jesus, who is the paradigm of the Christian life. Before doing that, he appeals to the affective faculties of his audience, who are to pattern their lives on Christ. Having already referred to the compassion (*splangchna*) of Christ in 1:8, the general appeal here must also certainly refer to the compassion of Christ as well as that of the community. This interpretation is strengthened by Paul's choice of second word to balance the statement, *oiktirmoi*, part of a word group often associated with the loving mercy of God (e.g., Exod 34:6; Deut 4:31; Neh 9:17; Isa 63:15; Pss 50 (51):3; 85 (86):15; 102 (103):8; Luke 6:36; Rom 12:1; 2 Cor 1:3; Jas 5:11). He appeals, then, not only to the compassion and sympathy of his audience, but to their participation *(koinōnia)* in those qualities of God and Christ.

Verse 2 is the consequence of the conditional statements of verse 1. Joy, a major underlying theme of the letter, is used as an appeal: "You want me to be happy? Well, this is how you can do it. . . ." The basic premise is indicated by the multivalent verb, *phronein*. It means more than "to think"; it is, rather, to have an attitude or orientation. They are to have the same attitude, to be oriented toward one and the same thing. They can do this by loving the same thing and being *sympsychoi,* or of the same *psychē,* personality or temperament, to be of one soul; in Latin-derived words, to be unanimous.

In verse 3 Paul warns the Philippians about unworthy motives that they could have in the situation that is causing the problem of disharmony among them. First, he asks them to do nothing from *eritheia,* which, as we have previously seen (1:17), is terminology drawn from conventional exhortations to civic harmony and usually implies malice of intention. The second negative term is *kenodoxia,* a much more colorful word than can be rendered in the single translation "conceit." One meaning is delusion, to let oneself be carried away into false thinking, but probably its wider meaning is at work here. The root is from two words, *kenos* (empty) and *doxa* (opinion or appearance). In this highly competitive social world, in which maintaining one's honor consists largely of keeping up appearances so as to be praised and esteemed by others, having an inflated but empty opinion of oneself and presenting a false appearance speak to the compulsion to be thought well of regardless of whether there is substantive quality of character to match the appearance.

Such a false shell with empty content is contrasted to *tapeinophrosynē,* humility, that encourages the countercultural attitude of seeing oneself as insignificant. The *tapeinos* is one who, originally, etymologically, is pressed down, thus oppressed. Through a semantic evolution, it came to acquire the meaning of voluntary lowliness. There is a significant difference in English between "humility" and "humiliation." These two meanings may be very close to each other here and in other such discussions arising from an honor-based culture. The hearers are not only to be lowly or humble, but to endure humiliation, which goes completely against the grain of a culture in which status is everything. This elusive connection between humility and humiliation is reinforced by the example of Jesus in the passage that follows. They are even to consider or esteem others comparatively as of superior status to themselves (*hyperechontes;* surpassing). Elsewhere in the letter Paul uses the same adjective in a superlative and positive meaning of knowing Christ (3:8) and of the peace of God that surpasses human understanding (4:7).

There could hardly be a more difficult challenge to a successful Greek or Roman male who considers himself to be someone important whom others will regard this way. Paul's references to suffering at 1:29 could involve the experience of being put down. Here he asks them to take upon themselves voluntarily the kind of attitude that will give honor to others rather than to self. The same thought is continued in verse 4, in which they are to look toward what will serve the best interests of others rather than themselves. These kinds of ideals are not unique. They are part of a traditional rhetorical vocabulary by which citizens were encouraged to pool their resources for the common good, usually without much success, to judge by the frequency of the discussions. But a different perspective will be introduced in what follows.

◊   ◊   ◊   ◊

The ideal of cooperation put forward here must be understood within the worldview of the first-century Mediterranean culture, not from twentieth-century psychology. Paul is talking about public and social behavior, not the crisis of self-image, self-love, and search for identity that are part of the contemporary individualist and introspective culture of the West. To "regard others as better than yourselves" might not be a healthy modern psychological ideal, but Paul's audience understood it as the conduct of yielding to another without fear of losing esteem by others.

THE BEST EXAMPLE: PHILIPPIANS (2:5-11)

Probably more has been written about this passage than any other New Testament passage with the possible exception of the Johannine Prologue, and the discussion of it continues unabated. Both stand out as unusual examples of early Christology. In both cases, for whatever point an author wishes to make, the exact opposite point can be readily found in other commentaries. The text of this passage in Philippians is therefore something of a minefield, full of implications likely to cause explosive reactions where least expected.

It is important to establish the place of the passage within the letter as a whole, its genre, and its internal structure. There are two points to be made about the place of the passage in context. First, most analyses of the structure of the letter see this passage as the first example given to the Philippians of how they are to conduct themselves in order to bring about unity. Second, it has a certain parallelism with Paul's example of himself in chapter 3, which is the second or third example, depending on whether one sees the function of the discussion of Timothy and Epaphroditus in 2:19-30 as second example or interlude between examples.

While the passage is frequently mined for its christological treasure, that is probably not why Paul chose to put it in the letter. Its entire context is parenetic, not doctrinal. It is part of the long central section of the letter from 1:27 to 2:18 in which Paul exhorts the Philippians to unity through humility and submission. He does not intend to teach Christology except inasmuch as Christ is the first and best example of what the audience could be like. The entire purpose is to persuade the audience that they must give up their own preferences for the sake of the other.

The genre of the text is certainly poetic. It has become customary to call it a "hymn" after some of the older classical religious hymns to major deities. It exhibits a certain rhythm, but not the meter characteristic of these older hymns (Basevi and Chapa 1993, 341). And of course we know absolutely nothing as to how or whether such a text was actually put to music. Beginning at verse 6, there is a natural tripartite structure of six stanzas, five of them starting at the opening of verses 6, 7, 9, 10, and 11. The exception is that the third stanza begins with the last clause of verse 7, "And being found in human form." This stanza thus contains four lines rather than three, which breaks the parallelism and has led some commentators to suppose the last of its lines, "even death on a cross," to be Paul's own interpolation in a previously composed piece, added because of his own emphasis on cross theology. Though the topic and thus the passage begins in verse 5 or 6, the rhythm of the lines begins at verse 6. The composition clearly concludes at the end of verse 11.

Preexistent Text?

There is general consensus that this is a "precomposed" text, that is, either Paul or more likely someone else composed it at a prior time, and Paul cites it to demonstrate his point. That consensus is sometimes questioned by rhetorical analysis that finds the passage perfectly harmonized with its context (e.g., Basevi and Chapa 1993). As was pointed out above, however, the structure of the lines in verses 6-11 is quite different from that of their surroundings. Like other poetic passages in the New Testament (John 1:1-18; Eph 2:14-16; Col 1:15-20; 1 Tim 3:16; 2 Tim 2:11-13; Titus 3:4-7; 1 Pet 3:18-22), it may have been composed for a liturgical setting, especially baptism or eucharist. That it fits so well into the text is rather due to Paul's compositional skill, or that of his secretary. (We know that Paul sometimes enlisted the help of a scribe not only to take his dictation but probably even sometimes to assist in the composition of the letter; see Rom 16:22; Gal 6:11).

This passage would form an appropriate backdrop to the Pauline interpretation of baptism as incorporation into the death of Jesus in order to share in his resurrection (Rom 6:2-11). Another kind of possible liturgical context is supplied by an outsider's remark about what Christians do when they assemble. Pliny the Younger as governor of Bithynia about half a century later (c. 110 CE) reported to his superior, the emperor Trajan, that he was investigating the group who called themselves Christians. Among other harmless things that they do, he reports, they assemble very early in the morning, before dawn, to "sing hymns to Christ as if to a god" (Pliny, *Letters* 10.96.7). Our text would fill that description quite nicely. It is likely that both Paul and the Philippians were familiar with the lines. If it was sung, they may have hummed along as that part of the letter was read!

Again as with the Johannine Prologue, theories of origin of the hymn extend from hellenistic mythology with no touch of Judaism, to Jewish-Christian-Gnostic, to completely Jewish and biblical, an indication of how universal were some of the language and symbolism contained in it, and also an indication as to how confusing and confused has been recent scholarship about it. Theories that have endured more than most can be broken into two categories. It was principally Käsemann who argued for a hellenistic environment in which the Greco-Roman converts were beginning to appropriate their own symbols into the formation of an entirely new kind of liturgical tradition. Focusing more on the second part of the passage, he presented the hymn as a mythological drama of a heavenly redeemer who is not posed as example, but rather as protological figure in whom believers are mystically incorporated.

The other major line of interpretation as to the origins of the hymn is that it is primarily drawn from Jewish-Christian and especially biblical sources, even perhaps originally composed in Hebrew or Aramaic. The possibility of translation from another language is generally not accepted. The text gives every evidence of having been composed in Greek. This does not exclude a Jewish origin, however, since many hellenistic-Jewish texts were written in Greek.

Biblical scholarship in the earlier part of this century was heavily influenced by new discoveries of parallels between biblical motifs and hellenistic religion. The theme of a heavenly figure who descends into the world with a salvific mission, and after accomplishing that mission ascends once more to heavenly exaltation is common to some hellenistic religious heroes, Gnostic mythology, the Johannine Prologue, and the Philippian hymn. More recent thinking has tended to emphasize the biblical background and origins of the language and thought world of the passage.

Preexistent Christ?

A bewildering number and variety of theories of interpretation can be sorted out under the familiar question: To be or not to be? Preexistent, that is. Before examining the passage in detail, we need to clarify some terminology. "Preexistent" in this context means that a being had some kind of extramortal existence before entering the realm of time and space and mortality. This does not necessarily imply divinity in the absolute sense, or humanity. In the Wisdom literature, the personified figure of Wisdom is usually presented as the first creation of God, who then assists in the rest of creation before entering into the people whom God chooses (see, for example, Prov 8:22-31; Sir 24:3-12). Stories of angelic manifestation in human history imply the preexistence of the angel outside the realm of history before manifestation in a given time and place. Daniel's mysterious Son of Humanity (Dan 7:13-14), a heavenly being that appeared to be like a human, was given all power and authority by the one on the throne, a figure of God. This passage is often cited as a precursor of an early Christian preexistent Christ.

With regard to Christology, the term "preexistence" means that Christ (Paul) or the Word-Logos (John) existed before becoming human as Jesus of Nazareth. It is not possible here to discuss all the early variations on Christology. In summary, within the first four centuries of the church, theologians and worshipers tried out various understandings of how that could be. At one extreme was the belief in the simple human birth of Jesus who was later taken over or adopted by the Logos at some point, perhaps at his baptism or resurrection (adoptionism). At the other end of the spectrum was the belief that Christ was so divine that he could not possibly be human, but presented only the appearance of humanity (docetism). Somewhere in the middle is what came to be orthodox belief as formulated in the Councils of Nicea (325 CE) and Chalcedon (451 CE): that the eternal Word of God was fully divine, always existed, yet entered completely into humanity in the person of Jesus, thus uniting full divinity and full humanity in the Incarnation.

The middle of the first century is long before these conciliar definitions of the fourth and fifth centuries, however. Their teaching can be read into the text, but the question to ask is whether these beliefs were present so early in the development of Christology. The traditional and still predominant view is that the hymn speaks of a heavenly (not necessarily divine) being who existed in the presence of God before the "emptying" of verse 7, which is usually interpreted as incarnation, or becoming human. Let us first read the passage from this perspective, at the same time examining some of the terminology and concepts in more depth.

Verse 5 is the introductory statement, probably written by Paul, that bids the Philippians to have a certain attitude, orientation, or mind-set, using the same verb *(phronein)* that was used twice in the appeal to unity in verse 2. Here in verse 5, the appeal to unity is not so direct, but the audience would undoubtedly make that connection by hearing the repetition of the verb, which is often lost in translation but is retained in the NRSV: "be of the same mind," "being . . . of one mind" in verse 2; "Let the same mind be in you" in verse 5. There are two ways to understand the latter part of the verse. The usual and traditional way is what is given in the NRSV main text: "Let the same mind be in you *that was in Christ Jesus,*" that is, imitate the attitude that Christ himself had, to be elaborated upon in the verses that follow.

Another way of understanding the sentence, however, is indicated in the NRSV note that would make the sentence read: "Let the same mind be in you *that you have* in Christ Jesus." "In Christ Jesus" is Paul's frequent way of referring to community life lived under the inspiration of the Spirit, incorporated into the mystery of the dying and rising of Christ. In this case, the sentence means "Set your attitude to be attuned to the best quality you have learned in your life in Christ Jesus," and imitation of the example of Jesus is not suggested. This is a minority interpretation that undermines the exemplary nature of the passage and would thus force a different understanding of the whole structure of the letter.

The hymn proper begins at verse 6 with three lines to the first stanza. Christ is described as being "in the form of God" *(morphē theou)*. The NIV translation "being in very nature God" overstates the traditional interpretation. *Morphē* is not "nature" as understood in later christological controversy, but form, shape, or appearance, with the understanding that that form expresses something of the reality it presents. Its use here stands in contrast to verse 7*b*, the *morphē* of a slave. The traditional interpretation of a preexistent Christ takes this to mean either an exalted heavenly figure very close to God or as full divinity. This interpretation is enhanced by the rest of verse 6: he did not consider it a *harpagmos*, something to be seized upon or exploited, to be *isa theō*, equal or of equal status to God.

Harpagmos presents an interpretive problem, since it is a relatively rare word, and when used, most often means "robbery" or "something that has been robbed," which it is most unlikely to mean here. Most translators and commentators move in the direction of the semantic area of exploitation to render the word. Christ could have exploited his position by misusing it to seek his own power or by remaining impassive in the face of his potential mission that would require grave inconvenience on his part. He could have just enjoyed his comfortable position and given no heed to that to which he was called.

The expression *isa theō* also requires some comment. The adjective *isos* means generally "equal" in the way that such a concept would have been understood within the context of the culture. The grammatical form here is a neuter plural used adverbially with a dative of comparison, a usage attested in classical authors. The word can be used to describe equality of size, shape, or mass of material objects. When applied to persons in this very status-conscious culture, it is more likely to mean equality of status or importance in a hierarchical order. It is not likely to mean what modern interpreters would want to read into the hymn, namely, equality of nature or substance with God. In other words, it is not a metaphysical but a social statement. Nevertheless, the traditional interpretation would see in the assertion that equality with God means virtually to be God.

The next stanza comprises the first three lines of verse 7. The verb of emptying, *ekenōsen,* is modified by the intensive reflexive *heauton,* himself. Thus the sense is active, not that Christ was emptied or humiliated, but that by his own choice he performed this action. The question is, What does this emptying mean? The next two lines give the answer: he took on himself the form (*morphē,* in contrast to the form of God in the previous verse) of a slave, which means "being born in human likeness." In contrast to the status and quality of God, he freely took on the far inferior status of humanity by becoming incarnate. Thus humanity is compared to the state of slavery. The status of being freeborn was highly prized by those who had it, but there was much philosophical musing about what really made one free or enslaved. Often the conclusion was that the passions are what enslaves, not one's legal status, so that the slave who had mastered the passions could be freer than the freeborn person who was enslaved to his or her own desires. All of these associations probably enter into play here. To take the form of a slave, here to become human, means to become subject to the domination of forces both exterior and interior that deprive one of freedom.

To take that idea a step further, people of the ancient Mediterranean world, like many people today, saw themselves as subject to hostile powers of the spirit world, especially those residing in the sky and able to control human destiny. This background is also suggested by the three-layered universe over which

Christ finally is raised in verses 9-10. Paul elsewhere speaks of human existence without faith in Christ as slavery to the elemental powers (Gal 4:8-9; cf. Rom 8:15; also Col 2:18). This too was part of becoming human. The one who was far superior to all these superhuman spirits became just as subject to them as everyone else (Karris 1996, 53-54).

The next stanza begins at verse 7c (v. 8a in the RSV) and continues through verse 8. After the repetition of the word *morphē* in verses 6-7, two different words with the general meaning of "likeness" or "appearance" are used in verse 7b-d, *homoiōsis* and *schēma*. To try to make distinctions among the three is a fruitless exercise in hair-splitting. *Homoiōsis* perhaps carries a bit more connotation of external resemblance or likeness, *schēma* of bearing or comportment, but all three have little difference in their meaning. More fruitful is a closer look at the expression, "he humbled himself" *(etapeinōsen heauton)*. Recall the discussion of the virtue of *tapeinophrosynē* at 2:3 and the problematic distinction between humility and humiliation. Here in verse 8, the related verb is used, and considering where the thought will lead by the end of verse 8, it can be asked whether the true translation should be that he "humbled himself" or "humiliated himself." The contrast between this self-humbling and consequent exaltation by God (v. 9a) is the key to the movement of the hymn.

The impact of this self-humbling is that the one who was of equal status with God became obedient. Obedience is a relational concept: to whom was he obedient? The usual answer is God, which then carries the implication that God willed the death of Jesus. We are reminded of the Synoptic presentation of his agony in the garden before his arrest, in which he struggled with submission to God's will in spite of his own human resistance. But God is not named in this verse, and it is also possible that the necessary death of God's son is not part of the theology in this passage, but rather a general sense of obedience to human limitations, mortality being the greatest of these limitations. Romans 5:19 suggests that the obedience of Jesus serves as antidote to the disobedience of Adam and was thus redemptive. Hebrews 5:7-8 evokes the scene in Gethsemane and suggests that Jesus learned obedience as a result of suffering, like a son tested by his father to develop strength of character in him. More will be said about this below when an alternate interpretation of the hymn is given.

The obedience of Jesus goes all the way to the point of death, the supreme paradox for a heavenly, immortal, preexistent being, and total nonsense for God. But the obedience and the death should not be separated: death is the content of the obedience. Verse 8c makes this obedience even more explicit: it is death on a cross. Because this line breaks the threefold pattern of the rest of the composition, it is sometimes thought to be Paul's own interpolation. Structural patterns aside, however, it completes and deepens the thought of what went before. For an immortal, preexistent being, death is bad enough. But for anyone, one of the worst kinds of death that could have been imagined in Greco-Roman antiquity was crucifixion.

Used as a method of executing criminals, slaves, and enemy captives, the practice of crucifixion spread from Persians to Greeks to Romans. The keynote of this manner of execution is shame. The victim was publicly paraded through the streets, inviting ridicule from bystanders, completely stripped, and fastened by ropes or nails in a very uncomfortable and completely defenseless posture in full view until death by asphyxiation and exposure, sometimes occurring several days later. (The six hours of Jesus' agony on the cross narrated by Mark 15:25, 34 was rather fast.) Normally the bodies of the crucified were left exposed to be eaten by birds or animals, the remnants to be buried in a common pit, unless someone had the clout to obtain release of the body for private burial (see Matt 27:57-58; Mark 15:43-45; John 19:31). The lack of dignified burial added to the humiliation and shame for the victim and his or her family. Death by crucifixion was considered to deprive the victim of all honor and submerge him or her—for women were also crucified—in shame. Once again, the reversal of status is at issue here: the one of equal status with God dies, and dies a most shameful death (see, e.g., Hengel 1977).

The threefold line structure picks up again at verse 9 and continues through the end of verse 11. Verse 9 is the turning point of the narrative. A clear cause-effect relationship between the first and second parts is suggested. It is *because* Jesus voluntarily lowered himself that God raised him up. The downward movement is now sharply reversed into a steep climb. God not only exalted him, but also bestowed on him a new name that reigns supreme above all other names, but apparently one that he did not have before. What is this name? If it is Jesus, as suggested by verse 10*a*, it is difficult to reconcile the giving of this historical name with the moment of exaltation. It fits better if the name is either Lord or Christ (messiah), as in verse 11; see the juxtaposition of these two titles in the christological proclamation of Acts 2:36.

The title "Lord" seems to have been highly significant in early Christian creed and liturgy: see the stress on this title in 1 Cor 12:3. The title need not be understood with the maximalist interpretation suggested early in this century, whereby, because the Greek *kyrios* was used in place of the sacred name of God in the LXX, its use by Paul suggested equation of Jesus with the creator God of the Hebrew Scriptures. But it did mean for Paul and other Christians of his day the positioning of the Risen Christ at God's right hand, the second most powerful position in the kingdom. The opening lines of Ps 110, "The LORD says to my lord, 'Sit at my right hand until I make your enemies your footstool,'" were freely interpreted in early Christian preaching to refer to the exaltation of Christ.

The title of Christ, that is, God's anointed one or the Messiah, is important not only for Paul but for the Synoptic writers as well. In an original Jewish context, the identification of Jesus as Messiah was highly controversial and even seditious. In Paul's letters addressed mostly to Gentiles, it is puzzling that he uses it so much. For Paul, it seems that this title has become part of Jesus' name, similar to modern usage. It does not seem as likely that the proclamation of Jesus as Christ is the point of the assertion. The structure of the statement suggests emphasis on the first title, Lord. Nearly all translations see it that way. All must confess that Jesus the Messiah is now Lord, that is, the one at God's right hand.

This piece is difficult to explain from the perspective of preexistence and incarnation. What more could be added that this heavenly being did not have before? Perhaps the answer is the triumph of the resurrected humanity of Christ, a new reality in divine existence.

The effect of this exaltation and gifting by God is expressed in verses 10-11. The poetic figure of all knees bending and all tongues acclaiming echoes Isa 45:23 and evokes a transhistorical throne room scene like Rev 4:2-11. The scenario embraces the three dimensions of human imagination at the time. The earth is mortal reality. Above the earth is the realm of spirits and gods and, according to some beliefs, those mortals who have been raised to immortality in the stars. Below the earth is the realm of death. So those alive, those deceased, and all superhuman spirits must acclaim the superiority of this great one who has been raised far above them by God. Even though the shamed crucified Jesus is now exalted Lord, thus being honored way beyond expectation, the ultimate honor belongs to God who pulled it off (v. 11c). God's honor above all is vindicated in the triumph of the exalted Christ.

Thus far, we have been looking at the hymn in detail, but also with the general perspective of the traditional interpretation whereby it speaks of the preexistence of Christ before his incarnation as Jesus of Nazareth. Some would see the equality with God as an early affirmation of the divinity of Christ. Unfortunately our word "divinity" is inexact. In Greek cosmology, including hellenistic Judaism to some extent, there are many levels of divinity. The one God is sole and unique, but there are various kinds of heavenly beings who share certain qualities of divine existence, and there are some with human origins who were raised to divine existence (Hercules, Dionysus, and others). Philippians 2:6 does not say that Christ was God, in the way that John 1:1 asserts of the Logos, but instead uses status language, "on the same level with" God. The emptying and taking the form of a slave is becoming human, which necessarily involves death. Even within the traditional interpretation, divinity in the absolute sense is probably not being ascribed to Christ, but rather, exaltation to the divine realm to share the status and qualities of God.

In recent years, a somewhat different interpretation has been suggested, based largely on the difficulty already raised at verse 9, that Christ is there, to all appearances, raised to a new status that he did not have before. This verse does not fit smoothly with a paradigm of preexistence. Those who therefore look for a different explanation find it in discussions in the intertestamental period of the relationship between sin and death and new interpretations of the transgression of Adam as narrated in Gen 3, with Adam increasingly being seen as the typological human being. Wisdom 2:23-24 sums it up nicely: "God created us for incorruption, and made us in the image of his own eternity, but through the devil's envy death entered the world, and those who belong to his company experience it."

Paul picks up this interpretation in Rom 5:12-21: sin came into the world through the sin of disobedience of one man, Adam, and death came as a result of sin, then spread throughout the human race because of the continued sin of all. The first human beings, in other words, were created immortal and were never intended to die. Death came only through their sin and continues to their descendants who reinforce the situation with their own sin. God's threat that the first man and woman would die if they ate of the forbidden tree (Gen 2:17; 3:3) was not a threat of retaliation but a prediction.

Joined to this background is Paul's statement in 2 Cor 5:21 that for our sake God made the one who knew no sin to be sin so that we might become righteousness—a puzzling passage. It speaks of the idea that Christ was sinless, a commonly accepted christological affirmation. But what does it mean that he was made to be sin? These considerations and others like them lead to the alternate interpretation that the Philippian hymn is not about preexistence at all but about Christ's voluntary assumption of mortality from the moment of his birth.

A reading of the text through this lens produces some different conclusions. In verse 6, his being in the "form of God" and being of the same status as God do not refer to preexistence but to the immortality that was ours and his by right until the sin of Adam destroyed it (see Wis 2:23). Then the emptying in verse 7a is not a transformation from divine to human status, and the form of a slave that he assumes is not humanity, an idea that goes so against the grain of the doctrine of our creation in God's image. Rather, both refer to his free embrace of mortality, the effect of sin that he, the sinless one, did not inherit and did not have to accept. He took on the full apparatus of humanity including corruptibility (v. 7b-c), and his lowering of himself to death, even death on a cross (v. 8), spells out all the implications of that free acceptance of mortality that he took on for our sake. Then the exaltation (vv. 9-11) is more easily explained: the humanly born Jesus Messiah, because of his obedience not in becoming human, the only thing he was, but in embracing "the full catastrophe" of death, was raised up by God into the heavenly realm, seated at God's right hand (Ps 110:1), where he was given all power and authority (Dan 7:13-14; see Matt 28:18). Whether this newer interpretation will stand the test of time remains to be seen.

◊ ◊ ◊ ◊

Because Christ took on voluntary humbling, God exalted him. The first shall be last, the last shall be first. Those who lose their life will find it. We are here at the heart of the Christian passover mystery, from suffering to triumph, from death to life. This is the Christianized form of the dynamic that inspires the oppressed in every generation. In the Hebrew Scriptures, it is God who watches out for the interests of the poor and oppressed and brings them redress. With the addition of Christology, Jesus becomes the prototype of how that happens, and the slave becomes the prototype of the Christian. If Christ could become a slave, then the slave could image Christ. In the humiliation of Christ is the exaltation of the oppressed.

The traditional interpretation of the hymn to represent very early belief in the preexistence of Christ is more in harmony with the fully developed Christology of the fourth and fifth centuries. To reject this meaning for the Philippian hymn is not to say that such Christology could not already have been developing. Paul's passing reference at 1 Cor 8:6 to "one Lord, Jesus Christ, through whom are all things and through whom we exist," also probably the citation of a piece of liturgical poetry, already hints at the assimilation of Christ to the figure of Wisdom or to the biblical and philosophical Logos, agent of God's creation, images that will be much more developed later in such passages as Col 1:15-20 and the Johannine Prologue.

The question is rather what is intended in this text of Philippians by its author, its liturgical users, and Paul in his letter. To see the Philippian hymn as affirmation not of Christ's preexistence but of his assumption of mortality changes the emphasis from protology, or speculation about origins, to eschatology and concern about the future of humanity. There was a variety of Christologies in the New Testament and early church. Each contributed something to the long path of theological reflection that later became orthodox faith.

A further question of interpretation hinges on whether what is said about Christ in the hymn is meant to be held up as an example for those who are incorporated into him in baptism so that they carry on the pattern of life of the one who has been made Lord of and for them. This is the so-called "ethical" interpretation that has held sway with a majority of interpreters and is assumed in most commentaries for the general reader. It is also the interpretation that lends itself most naturally to a rhetorical analysis of the structure of the letter, such as that presented in the introduction to the volume and carried through in nontechnical terms throughout the commentary.

Toward the middle of this century, another interpretation, the "kerygmatic," was put forth notably by Ernst Käsemann, who argued that the hymn represents a kerygmatic proclamation and celebration of what Christ has done for us, but carries no exemplary import by which Christ is presented as model for imitation. Rather, by the very nature of our incorporation into Christ in baptism, we share in this mystical dying and rising, with no immediate connection to our deeds or attitudes. (A good summary of the two views can be found in O'Brien 1991, 253-62.) This interpretation must assume a pre-Pauline composition, for within the context of the letter alone, it would be very difficult to sustain. It also assumes much less a biblical than hellenistic religious background, the theme of the descending/ascending savior.

The assumption of a pre-Pauline existence of the hymn need not necessarily be connected with this interpretation. But we are brought back to the question: What was the intention and understanding of the author, the users, and Paul? We will never have sure answers about the first two. It is quite possible to suppose that the composer and regular users of the hymn, especially if it was used for baptismal liturgy, did not intend exemplary impact but saw it as a proclamation of the effects of incorporation into the now-exalted Christ. The pattern of his humiliation/exaltation would be their destiny, without emphasis on what they were to do during the process. But it is extremely difficult to look at the use of the hymn in the letter and think that Paul does not intend proposing the obedience of Jesus as a model to be imitated. Rather, Paul has taken a familiar piece and informed it with new and expanded meaning.

ENHANCING THE SACRIFICE THROUGH OBEDIENCE (2:12-18)

The mention of Christ's obedience at verse 8 fits perfectly with Paul's strategy in his use of the hymn in the letter. Regardless of the interpretation with regard to preexistence or immortality, the result is clear: God exalted Christ because of his obedience. Now in verse 12, Paul can appeal to the Philippians to follow the example of Christ by appealing to their long-standing pattern of heeding his wishes. This is good rhetorical style, to flatter with praise while encouraging listeners to do more. The Philippians are Paul's allies and disciples whether he is there or only wishing to be there (see also 1:27). The words for "presence" and "absence," somewhat alliterative in English, create a neat play on words in Greek: *parousia* and *apousia*. The first word is of course familiar for the specialized meaning that was beginning to take shape even in Paul's vocabulary (1 Thess 4:15), the final eschatological arrival of the exalted Christ. Here it is used in its general sense of "presence" or "arrival."

The "fear and trembling" is a biblical expression that appears with a certain frequency in the LXX (e.g., Exod 15:16; Deut 2:25; 11:25; Ps 2:11; Isa 19:6; 4 Macc 4:10). The fact that it is used in the Ephesian household code to describe the obedience of slaves (Eph 6:5) suggests that it has become a conventional expression (see also 1 Cor 2:3; 2 Cor 7:15).

The greater difficulty is the idea of working at salvation in an active sense. Salvation, *sōtēria,* carries the general sense of health, welfare, and well-being, and especially protection and deliverance from danger. It is what an effective ruler is expected to provide for his or her subjects, and one who does is often proclaimed *sōtēr,* savior, as was Augustus, for example. In hellenistic religion before its Christian use, the word also acquired some meaning of individual salvation beyond mortal life, though exactly how this was conceived is vague. Use of the word here is certainly not to be understood only in the eschatological sense, as if only a state beyond death is envisioned, yet that dimension must be included. Paul is speaking of their total well-being, including their spiritual prosperity both now and in the future.

This multidimensional meaning is also present in the other two uses of the word in this letter. At 1:19, Paul expresses his hope that he will be freed from imprisonment by quoting Job 13:16, which carries a similar meaning. That will be his salvation, just as deliverance from afflictions will be salvation for Job. The NRSV translates "deliverance" in Phil 1:19 and "salvation" in Job 13:16, but the same word is used. In 1:28, the meaning turns more toward an ultimate state cast in dualistic terms of ultimate success or failure. In both 1:28 and 2:12, the modifiers are plural. It is not so much individual salvation as communal eschatological success that is envisioned. This is not to deny the individual aspects of the concept, but neither Paul nor his contemporaries thought primarily in individual terms. The collective good is the principal referent.

Verses 14-16 contain conventional parenesis with many conventional terms: "murmuring" (or grumbling) and "arguing," "blameless and innocent," "children of God," "without blemish," in a "crooked and perverse generation." Conventional terms, but not necessarily familiar Pauline terms: "murmuring" *(gongysmos)* and "without blemish" *(amōmos)* do not occur elsewhere in the authentic Pauline letters. The whole description, however, evokes the "murmuring" of the Israelites in the desert, especially a comparison with Deut 32:5, where the "crooked and perverse generation" is described in almost identical terms in the LXX. Whether the Gentile Philippians would recognize the allusion is questionable, unless they had already been well schooled in Exodus traditions and were familiar with the text of Deuteronomy, but Paul the Pharisaic scholar could hardly help using descriptions familiar to him to describe a similar situation.

Is the situation in Philippi really that similar? This raises again the question that we must circle around throughout the letter: Just what is going on in Philippi that Paul feels he has to comment on, and what does he know about it? The analogy with exodus traditions would suggest sedition against legitimate leadership and rebellion against God. In verse 12, Paul has introduced the idea of obedience, presumably to him, but perhaps there is more to the story. A rebellion against local leadership may well be part of the problem, and that may be why Paul included in the ascription of the letter those with leadership titles (1:1), to draw the attention of all at Philippi to his support for them.

Their reward for unity and obedience without grumbling is laid before them in an image whose language evokes Dan 12:3. The reference must be understood on two levels, or with two possible meanings to be held in tension with each other. "You shine" *(phainesthe)* in verse 15 is present tense, so that the passage may be linked to the idea behind Matt 5:14-16, and the shining that they do "in the world" is here and now. Thus the intent is missionary: they will win outsiders by their good example. But the similarity to the passage in Daniel suggests something more. There the verb is future tense and an eschatological venue is intended. Daniel refers to the common apocalyptic intertestamental belief, probably drawn from hellenistic mysticism, that the reward of the just is to be enthroned resplendently in the heavenly realm with the angels. That is to say, the declaration that if faithful, they will also in the future "shine like stars in the world" is not a simile but a promise. This was one way of envisioning exaltation at death, or resurrection (cf. Matt 22:30). The word *world (kosmos)* does not appear in Daniel, who instead uses *ouranos* (sky). A different and definitely more eschatological impression would be conveyed if *kosmos* were translated here not as "world" but as "cosmos," a term in English that is more closely associated with the world *above* than the world below.

The juxtaposition of *kosmos* at the end of verse 15 with *logos zōēs* (word of life) at the beginning of verse 16 has a curiously Johannine echo, which simply demonstrates that even though the terminology became characteristic of a specific context, it could be used in other theological contexts as well.

Paul's thought next turns to himself in verses 16-17, first to his missionary success with the Philippians, then once again to the uncertain outcome of his present situation (see 1:19-26). Though it is obscured in some translations, Paul here makes use of one of his expressions most troublesome to modern readers: boasting. He hopes to be able to boast "on the day of Christ," that is, in the eschatological reckoning, that his labor among them was a success. The language of boasting, which is frequent in the Pauline letters, often strikes modern readers as immodest and inappropriate. It is language of honor and shame. To be able to boast is to take pride in something or someone, and therefore not to be shamed by those who seek to deprive their opponents of honor. Paul is careful to refer that honor ultimately to Christ or God (see 1:27). Yet here there is an element of self-focus: when he stands before the judgment seat of Christ (2 Cor 5:10), he will not be ashamed.

There is also an element here of another thing that the modern reader often dislikes about Paul: he seems manipulative. To paraphrase verse 16*b-c*, if the Philippians do what he wants, he will be honored by Christ. If not, his honor is at risk—and it will be their fault. These are precisely the kinds of arguments employed by Paul out of his rhetorical skill, the kinds of arguments that were expected in order to sway a crowd in oral or written communication to persuade them to come around to where the speaker wants to lead them. To speak of success or failure, Paul uses an expression also used in Gal 2:2 to refer to the way in which he felt it necessary to check out his gospel with the "pillars" at Jerusalem. He does not want to have run in vain *(eis kenon)*, literally, "in emptiness" or perhaps in modern automotive parlance, "running on empty." Metaphors of emptiness were a favorite way to talk about uselessness, madness, and impotence (*1 Clem. 1* 7.2; Pol. *Phil.* 2:1; *Shepherd of Hermas Mandate* 11). The reference here is not without echoes of the voluntary emptiness of Christ in 2:7 and Paul's "loss" in 3:7.

Verses 17-18 pick up again the frequent refrain of rejoicing that is characteristic of the Philippian letter. A new metaphor is introduced that is rich in overtones of temple liturgy. Paul speaks of the possible sacrifice of his life as a libation of wine that is poured out on the altar or on a grave at a funerary banquet as a form of religious sacrifice. There is no need to think of the libation as his blood poured out in death, as is often thought. That interpretation takes the metaphor a further unnecessary step. But the analogy of being poured out is necessarily associated with the dissolution of death: compare 2 Tim 4:6; Ign. *Rom.* 2.2. The wine offering is to be poured out on the *thysia* (a word for temple sacrifice) and the *leitourgia* of their faith. This second word, from which the word "liturgy" derives, originally meant in the hellenistic city a compulsory public office that included some financial and religious function. That is probably the connotation that it still holds in Paul's time. He uses similar terminology in 2:25, 30 (see further comment there) and in Rom 15:16, where he speaks of himself as *leitourgos,* performer of *leitourgia* to the Gentiles and priest of the Gospel of God, so that the sacrificial offering of the Gentiles might be acceptable. In later Christian usage the word would come to mean public religious cult (see Horsley and Llewelyn 7:1994, 93-111).

It is doubtful both here and in Romans that Christian religious *worship* is meant—as distinct from Christian *faith*—for that connection has not yet developed and could not until Christians began to see themselves engaged in public action similar at least to that of the Jerusalem temple and other temples of other gods with which the cities of Paul's mission were filled. Nor do we have any evidence that at this early date the Eucharist, or Lord's Supper in Paul's terminology, was seen primarily as sacrifice and therefore intended here. In these letters, Paul is borrowing temple sacrificial language and employing it metaphorically. He does something similar in Rom 12:1, where we see that the whole of the Christian life is meant to function as a sacrifice rather than to focus on the act of worship.

◊ ◊ ◊ ◊

Several things in verse 12 have given rise to considerable controversy, notably Paul's appeal to obedience, and his admonition to the readers to work out their own salvation. In later denominational differences, these terms raised hackles about a "Jewish/Catholic" approach to salvation by works as opposed to a "Protestant" belief in salvation by faith alone. Let us remember that Paul was certainly Jewish, but neither Catholic nor Protestant, and try to approach the text from the perspective of a first-century Pharisaic messianic Jew. The statement must be seen as part of an ongoing thought carried further in verse 13. The obedience advocated here is not yet the radical submission to the gospel as it later came to be understood in Reformation theology. Paul is not posing to the Philippians the choice of obedience or destruction. He is simply reminding them that their submission to him on the issue at hand, the disunity in the community, will carry them further toward their spiritual welfare.

How are the Philippians to work out their own salvation? Is not salvation a free gift of God? While Paul certainly does make it clear elsewhere that salvation is the free gift of God's grace that cannot be earned, he is equally clear that life according to this gift of grace is life according to the Spirit in which there are certain behavioral expectations (e.g., Gal 5). God's covenant with Israel is a free gift that requires a response. In the same way, salvation in Christ means transformation into the new creation (*kainē ktisis*, 2 Cor 5:17; Gal 6:15), which means conversion of life. It is this appropriate and necessary response to the grace of God that is meant here by the injunction to work out your own salvation.

That interpretation is reinforced by verse 13: it is really God who is at work in believers.

PRAISE FOR TWO COWORKERS (2:19-30)

The function of this section in the structure of the letter is seen in several different ways, though it obviously serves as a transitional section between the exhortation to unity in 2:1-18 and the warning and autobiographical reflection of chapter 3. For some commentators Timothy and Epaphroditus together supply the second of three examples of self-submission for the good of the whole. The third will be Paul himself in chapter 3. For others, this section is an interlude between the two sections. (See the introduction for further discussion of the structure of the letter.)

◊　◊　◊　◊

This section is both newsy information about two of Paul's associates and their comings and goings to Philippi and at the same time high praise for each of them. Paul declares his intention soon to send Timothy, who is with him as he writes the letter (1:1), but not before he knows something more definite about the outcome of his own present situation (2:23). The visit will apparently be quick since the purpose is a fact-finding mission so that Timothy can report back to Paul (v. 19). More proximately, Epaphroditus is being sent back with the letter, not for a quick visit, but to stay, so Paul does not expect to receive back any news from him.

Timothy is one of the most frequent characters in the Pauline accounts. According to Acts, he was from Lystra in Asia Minor, the uncircumcised son of a Jewish mother and Greek father, well thought of and chosen by Paul as missionary companion, circumcised by Paul when his uncircumcised status was causing trouble (Acts 16:1-3). He appears with Paul in the prescript of several other letters (2 Cor 1:1; 1 Thess 1:1; Phlm 1) besides this one. A most trusted companion and assistant, Timothy may have been someone Paul could rely upon in difficult situations, since he was sent to Corinth at a time of considerable problems there (1 Cor 4:17). Both there and here at 2:22 Paul uses paternal imagery about him, an indication that Timothy is not only co-missionary but one who carries out Paul's wishes and is accountable to him. The positive memory of Timothy as trusted companion of Paul led to later pseudonymous letters, 1 and 2 Timothy, which placed him long-term in Ephesus (1 Tim 1:3; 2 Tim 1:18; 4:12), giving rise to a later tradition that he was the first bishop of that city.

The function of the reference to Timothy is more than the news that he will perhaps come to them. That piece of information is first put forth in verse 19 and repeated in verse 23. Those two references form an inclusion around the laudatory description of Timothy in the intervening verses. It does seem that this uncalled-for praise of someone who has not entered into the immediate story is put there for a definite purpose, and that purpose is to hold him up as example of someone who does not seek his own interests, but those of Christ (v. 21; cf. 2:4 where Paul admonishes the Philippians to do the same). Without needing to be told, Timothy seeks the interests of Christ and thus stands out "in the midst of a crooked and perverse generation" (v. 15), which they will also do if they follow suit. Timothy is therefore proposed as an exemplary model for the Philippians to follow.

Paul says of Timothy that he has no one "like him" (v. 20), a rather weak rendering of the rare word *isopsychos,* which occurs in biblical literature only here and in Ps 54:14 LXX (55:13). We have seen at 2:6 that *isos* carries the meaning of equality or close similarity of status. *Psychē* is the common term for "soul" or sometimes "mind," often used in compounds, for example in 2:2 where Paul asks the Philippians to be *sympsychoi,* thinking or feeling together. In the previous verse (v. 19), Paul has used another compound, *eupsychō,* a subjunctive verb meaning "to be encouraged or cheered," which is then played off alliteratively with this word. In Ps 54:14 (55:13) the context is that it is not an enemy but one who is *isopsychos* who has betrayed the speaker. Here the connotation is of a social equal, a companion and friend. The word is necessarily comparative: one has to be equal to someone or something. The likely comparison is with Paul himself. Everything we know about Timothy indicates that the two of them got on very well together and that Paul held him in great affection and esteem. In spite of the fact that Timothy "works for" Paul in the sense that Paul can send him on various missions, Paul sees Timothy as a "soul friend." This impression is reinforced by the next verse (v. 22) in which Paul says that Timothy has served with him, not served him, in the cause of the gospel.

Paul's complaint in verse 21 that everyone else looks after their own interests echoes a similar complaint at 1:15-17 about the unworthy motives of some believers and evangelizers. It serves as a foil to the words of praise for Timothy that surround it on both sides, and as the center of the inclusive structure that occupies verses 19-23. The filial simile of verse 22 uses not the word *huios* (son) but *teknon* (child), emphasizing the close, affectionate relationship rather than the status and legal issues of how father and son are expected to deal with each other. He speaks of Timothy in the same way in 1 Cor 4:17 (see also 1 Tim 1:2 and Paul's similar reference to Onesimus in Phlm 10).

Paul intends to send Timothy to them to represent himself and give him a report as soon as he knows how things will go for him in the crisis situation in which Paul finds himself. Verse 24 adds the hope that Paul himself will be able to return. Some commentators see contradictory meaning between this hope of survival, similar to that in 1:25, and the libation of his life at verse 17, and therefore conclude that the libation cannot refer to his death. But that possibility is hypothetical, and there is nothing strange about someone who does not know whether he will be killed or released thinking about both alternatives in close succession.

Verses 25-30 turn to the plight of Epaphroditus, who may or may not be the same as Epaphras (Col 1:7; 4:12; Phlm 23; see arguments pro and con in Horsley and Llewellyn 4:1987, 22-23). He brought to Paul in prison the gifts sent by the Philippians (4:18) and apparently intended to stay with Paul. But there is some problem here. Paul now feels constrained to send him back to Philippi where he will apparently arrive unexpectedly. Epaphroditus has been deathly ill (vv. 26-27), which Paul thinks would not have happened had he not been there doing the work of Christ (v. 30). He survived and is now out of danger. Paul is eager to praise him, calling him brother, coworker, and fellow soldier in the strife of the gospel. He makes clear that Epaphroditus has been of great help to him as *leitourgos* in his need; helping Paul is also Epaphroditus's *leitourgia* in verse 30 (see discussion of this term at 2:17). In verse 29 Paul gives a formal recommendation of him and requests that he be received well, speaking in the way one would of a stranger to be introduced (compare his recommendation of Phoebe in Rom 16:1-2). But Epaphroditus is well known in Philippi, and probably comes from there. So why does Paul try so hard to justify Epaphroditus's return to Philippi?

Some commentators, seeing conflict everywhere in the letter, have read into this awkward situation that there is conflict between Paul and the Philippians with Epaphroditus in the middle of it, or that the tension is between Epaphroditus and his own community, with Paul in the middle trying to diffuse it. Neither interpretation is necessary. The situation is not conflict but social discomfort. There is one other term that Paul calls him, not yet commented upon. In verse 25, besides brother, coworker, fellow soldier, and minister *(leitourgos),* he also calls Epaphroditus "your *apostolos*," translated in the NRSV as "messenger." Like *episkopos, diakonos* (1:1), and *leitourgia* (2:17), this is another term with pre-Christian origins that came at a certain point to acquire a specific new meaning in Christian contexts.

Originally a designation for someone who carries a message or representative action from one party to another, already in the Pauline churches *apostolos* came to mean one officially delegated by a church to proclaim the gospel in a missionary capacity. (Luke alone also uses the term to designate the twelve in a particular way; we are not concerned here with this special Lukan usage.) Examples include Paul himself and others of his acquaintance: Rom 1:1; 11:13; 16:7; 1 Cor 1:1; 4:9; 9:1-2, 5; 12:28; 2 Cor 11:5, and many others. Once in a while in the New Testament, the context is sufficiently ambiguous that it is not clear whether the correct translation should be "apostle" or "messenger." Such is the case at 2 Cor 8:23, a rather vague reference to persons known to the Corinthians but not to us, "*apostoloi* of the churches," also translated "messengers" in the NRSV. Such is also the case here in 2:25 with Epaphroditus.

If instead of understanding him as a messenger, he is seen as an apostle, the meaning is clarified. Epaphroditus has gone off from Philippi, his home, to serve with Paul as an apostle. He is "your apostle," one sent out from the Philippian community with great pride. But he "didn't make the grade." Either his health or temperament or both was not suited to the life, so upon his recovery, Paul makes the difficult decision ("I think it necessary" [*anagkaion de hēgēsamēn*]) to send him back home. In the days without telephones, faxes, or E-mail, his appearance would be a total surprise. So in order to sweeten the hard decision, he praises Epaphroditus to the hilt, as any good administrator would, and asks the Philippians to take him back wholeheartedly. The news of Epaphroditus may be placed precisely here as one of the examples of selfless conduct along with Timothy, but there is more to the story than that.

Transition and Warning (3:1-4*a*)

Because our chapter and verse divisions, which were not part of the original composition, break between 2:30 and 3:1, it is difficult for modern readers to see that 3:1 really continues directly from the previous verse. The opening of verse 1 is one of the clearest pieces of evidence for those who would argue for a composite letter. It sounds like a conclusion of what went before and even a conclusion to a letter, especially if the first expression, *to loipon*, is translated "finally" as it often is. (See 2 Cor 13:11 where the same expression does indeed mark the end of the letter, but also 1 Cor 4:2; 7:29; 1 Thess 4:1; 2 Tim 4:8 where it does not.) It was pointed out in the introduction that there are other ways of understanding the term: as summary of a previous argument, but not necessarily as grand conclusion of everything. It is a way of moving on to another topic, which indeed Paul does in the following verses. At the same time, Paul again expresses a wish for their joy, following on verses 27-28, where he hopes that the return of Epaphroditus will bring them joy and that they will receive him in the same attitude. Now there is one more repetition of that wish in 3:1*a*.

Verse 1*b*, however, could face either way. It may be part of the conclusion of the previous discussion, or more likely it serves as introduction to the new topic that will begin in the next verse. In what has gone before, we do not get the impression that Paul is repeating himself, but the excoriation of verse 2 is familiar to any reader of Pauline letters. So the "same things" must have to do with what is coming, and what will be familiar to them because they so often heard those things from Paul himself and anyone else who represented him, such as Timothy or Epaphroditus. Most translators have problems with the next part of the sentence, literally: "It is not annoying to me, and it is safe *(asphales)* for you." The NRSV makes the final part a little more colloquial by rendering it as a "safeguard." Something in the semantic range of "good" or "beneficial" probably suggests the idea better.

If the above interpretation is correct, then the real break in thought is not between 3:1 and 3:2, but between 3:1*a* and 1*b*. Seen this way, the transition is not as rough as it is sometimes made out to be. Paul has just spoken of Epaphroditus and his hope that all can rejoice at his homecoming. He concludes that part by saying something like, "So now, be happy in the Lord." To change the subject, he then says in effect, "Now I am repeating myself in what comes next, but that's all right, and besides, it's good for you."

What is it that Paul now repeats? It is a warning apparently against people similar to his opponents in Galatians, those who would insist that circumcision and consequent observance of the whole ritual law are requisite for church membership. Such groups would probably be not other Jews but Jews who have joined the church. There are many difficulties here, not least of which is that, if this tension is a real problem at Philippi, this is the first and last time we hear about it. Considering the turmoil the issue created in Galatia, it is difficult to suppose that if Paul thinks the Philippians are threatened by it, he would dismiss the whole thing in a few verses. In spite of these difficulties, some commentators remain with the interpretation that this is indeed a problem at Philippi, and in very strong language, Paul warns them not to become entangled with it.

There are other possible solutions, however. Verse 2 consists of three short clauses, each introduced by *blepete,* a second-person plural indicative imperative of the verb "to see." Usual translations are "Beware of," "Look out for," and so on, in a tone of warning against danger. But there are other ways to understand the imperative. When intended as a warning, it is usually followed by a negative and an aorist subjunctive ("Beware lest . . .") or the preposition *apo* ("from") with the sense "Guard yourselves from. . . ." Neither is the case here, so the verbs could mean rather "Look to . . . ," or "Take, for example, . . ." as the same form does in 1 Cor 1:26; 10:18 (Keller 1995, 30; Stowers 1991, 116). In this case, verses 2-3 are a transition to the main point to which Paul is leading, his own credentials both in Israel and with regard to imitation of Christ and his cross. These are the themes that will be developed in the rest of the chapter.

The rhetorical function of the passage needs also to be taken into account. If it really is an abrupt departure from what went before, the quick turnabout is a device to create "shock value," a startling interlude between two heavy points. But rhetorical analysis suggests otherwise. To the extent that the letter is characterized by the tradition of friendship, the creation of bonds of friendship requires the construction of inimical outsiders to serve as contrast. As one author puts it, in the social and rhetorical world in which Paul moves, there are only three kinds of people: friends, enemies, and people you don't know (Stowers 1991, 113). Since the major appeal of the letter is for community unity (as, e.g., in 1 Cor 5:1-5), with no provision that anyone be left out or ejected from that unity, some enemy has to be proposed. It is unlikely that these "Judaizers" are present at Philippi though they have a very real existence in other places, especially Galatia. If Paul wants to pick some group that he can portray as enemies from past experience, this is it. They will serve as a foil to Paul himself with his own faultless credentials.

Still, there is a certain vehemence in the way Paul attacks these groups. It is the vehemence of conventional rhetoric in which there must be enemies to excoriate, and it is legitimate to accuse them of every abuse imaginable. Paul calls them by three epithets in a triple diatribe, all beginning with the Greek letter "kappa" for alliteration: *kynas, kakous ergatas,* and *katatomē,* "dogs," "evil workers," and "mutilators." For most ancient people, dogs were not pets but scavengers that fed on the remnants of banquets (Luke 16:21) and on garbage heaps. They were therefore irrevocably associated with uncleanness and filth, so it is no surprise that they were a pejorative Jewish term for Gentiles (Matt 7:6; 15:26-27; Mark 7:27-28). But it is unlikely that the referents here are Gentiles. Just the opposite. In this context we can catch the difference and horror of Paul's rhetorical angle. Those who pride themselves on their ritual purity are as unclean as are the Gentiles in their own estimation!

Any group branded as the enemy could be called evil workers. The expression may be a variant on a familiar reference in the Psalms to "workers of iniquity" (*hoi ergazomenoi tēn anomian,* LXX Pss 5:6; 6:8; 13:4; and others). But there may be more to the terminology than general vituperation. The word for "worker" (*ergatēs*) may by this time have had ministerial or missionary overtones as in Matt 9:37-38; 10:10; Luke 10:2, 7; 2 Tim 1:15; even negatively as in 1 Cor 11:13 of the so-called false apostles, and so refer to Christian missionaries who are unworthy of their calling. Another possibility is a connection with law observance. In Romans, Paul contrasts the efficacy of faith in Christ to that of works (*erga*) of the law that are connected with circumcision (e.g., in Rom 3:27-28). Thus the epithet "evil workers" (*kakous ergatas*) may be used for those who insist on law observance and circumcision for Gentile converts, as suggested by the third epithet, mutilators. (See a full discussion in O'Brien 1991, 355-56.) The first term, "dogs," was a sarcastic reversal of ordinary use, as the third will be also. It is therefore to be expected that this second term is used in the same way and will have the same impact (Fee 1995, 296).

The two possibilities named above, Christian missionaries and those who advocate law observance, are of course not mutually exclusive. One of Paul's major struggles in his ministry was against the position of Jewish Christians who believed, taught, and practiced that observance of the Mosaic law was necessary for full membership in the church. In view of the third term, "those who mutilate the flesh," or more literally, "the mutilation," it seems likely that both may be intended: Christian missionaries or preachers, whether Jew or Gentile, who preach circumcision and law observance for Gentile Christians, the same kind of group that is targeted in Galatians. As argued above, this does not mean that such a group was present in Philippi. They are the "ogres" whom Paul can draw upon to portray rhetorical contrast.

The third epithet is as sarcastic as the first. It will remind Pauline readers of Gal 5:12, where Paul wishes that his opponents, the same described above, once they had the knife, would just keep cutting themselves, a circumlocution for castration. The word for circumcision *(peritomē)* has the same etymology as the Latinate word "circumcision" used in English, "to cut around." But Paul's word for the opponents here is *katatomē*, a derogatory play on words, not "cut around" but "cut up" or mutilate. The play can work somewhat in English by translating "Beware of the mutilation. We are the circumcision." A more literal rendering of the contrast between the two terms would be viable if modern readers were aware of the literal meaning of circumcision, to cut around: "Beware of those who cut up. We are those who cut around." While this third epithet belongs to the triad of verse 2, it also looks forward to the next statement in the following verse.

Verse 3 is very difficult to explain in a Jewish context. It is characterized by Pauline language that is more at home in the disputes about the law in Galatians and Romans: boasting in Christ, spirit set against flesh, and especially the seemingly exclusive assertion to which Paul lays claim for the identity of the covenant people. We have already seen at 1:26 and 2:16 that "boasting" is a rhetorical device for the preservation of honor. It consists in establishing and maintaining claims to worth and appropriate qualifications. It is not inappropriate and immodest behavior but the necessary response to a challenge to one's honor. The connection between boasting and having confidence in this verse is very close, even though two different terms are used. One can only boast, that is, lay claim to honor, about the claims of which one is confident. At the beginning of verse 4, Paul lets us know that he too could be just as confident in the flesh, but chooses not to be so.

The contrast that Paul sets up is between those whose confidence is in their ritual observances and those whose confidence is in the gift of God in Christ. The first and negatively contrasted group is characterized therefore as those whose confidence is localized in the flesh, the site of ritual observance symbolized by circumcision. By contrast, the second group, represented by Paul, worship God not by ritual observance based in the flesh but by spiritual worship. It is important to remember in these kinds of discussions that ordinarily when Paul juxtaposes spirit and flesh, "flesh" does not mean body or matter. This is not a Gnostic context in which the goodness of matter is disparaged. For Paul, "flesh" is normally the innate tendencies that pull us away from life in the Spirit. That is clearest in Gal 5:16-26, where the works of the flesh and those of the spirit are partially enumerated. Here in 3:3, a slightly different twist is given that does not contradict Paul's usual use of spirit and flesh, but builds on it. He sees the claims of his opponents as inimical to the real service and worship of God, and so their practices do not carry observers to God but away from God. Because these are ritual observances, they can thus be doubly characterized as "flesh," a vain source of confidence and pride.

The most difficult statement in the verse, however, is the first: "We . . . are the circumcision." The way it is worded leaves no doubt that Paul is not suggesting, "We have a share in the circumcision," or something similar. It sounds like an absolute claim. We—whoever that is—are the only "circumcision." The expression refers to a social/religious group whose religious claims stem from their ritual observance, summed up in the act of circumcision (see the contrast between "circumcision" and "uncircumcision" in Gal 2:7 [these are the actual terms used in the text, in spite of the English participial translations "uncircumcised" and "circumcised"]). Here in Phil 3:3 Paul blurts out his statement with a sense of frustration recalling the opposition he has endured from this group. But the implication that can be drawn from the way the term "circumcision" is used here suggests that it is a substitute for the covenant, the very central identity of Israel as chosen people (cf. Gal 6:16: "Peace . . . upon the Israel of God").

Is Paul then making a claim for the unique legitimacy of Gentile Christianity against the whole of Israel, whose claims should be abolished? Although it is sometimes interpreted this way by overzealous Christian interpreters, that is probably not the case. Among the "we" must be included large numbers of Jews who believe in Christ. His quarrel is not with all of Israel, his own people, but only with those who would thwart his efforts to include the Gentiles by insisting that they must go the route of ritual observance in order to be legitimate participants of the covenant. Against them, he makes the claim that those who acknowledge Jesus as Messiah and put all their confidence in him rather than in ritual observance fulfill the true meaning and intention of circumcision at its best.

The kind of statement that Paul makes at the beginning of verse 3 is perhaps better understood in the context of another passage, 2 Cor 3:4-14. Here he again speaks of confidence in God because of Christ (3:4). He contrasts not flesh and spirit but letter and spirit, claiming that God has made him and others like him ministers *(diakonoi)* of a new covenant (3:6), given with even greater splendor than the first, which then becomes the old covenant (v. 14). The former covenant is not destroyed but transformed by the glory of the new one. Paul's statement, "We . . . are the circumcision," in Phil 3:3 can be understood in the same way. It goes without saying that Paul constructs his arguments for rhetorical effect, that it is not the Jews who are his opponents but specific groups of "Judaizers," and that any attempt to construct a picture of first-century Jewish practice from Paul's remarks would be an unjust caricature.

PAUL'S CLAIMS TO CONFIDENCE AND HONOR (3:4*b*-11)

After having proposed Christ Jesus as example of how to renounce one's own will rather than impose it on others (2:6-11), then holding up to the Philippians the superior apostolic qualities of Timothy and Epaphroditus (2:19-30), Paul now sets out to propose himself as example of what Christ can accomplish in someone who surrenders to the demands of the Cross. But first, he must establish his credentials for making such claims.

Verses 5-6 are characterized by brief energetic phrases of two or three words, with slightly more prolonged phrases in verse 6. After the initial "circumcised on the eighth day" in verse 5 follows a triadic statement of Paul's credentials in Israel, then a triadic statement of his religious positions, each part introduced by the preposition *kata*, "according to," followed by an accusative noun: *kata nomon, kata zēlon, kata dikaiosynēn*, according to law, zeal, and righteousness. The rest of the passage moves in more typical flowing prose.

Verse 7 is a brief whole sentence. Verses 8-11, usually broken up into two or more sentences in translation, are in Greek one large sentence whose syntax is very complex. Everything depends on one principal verb, *hēgoumai* ("I regard"), stated twice; once toward the beginning and once toward the end of verse 8. The first use of the verb includes most of verse 8: "I regard everything as loss because of the surpassing value of knowing Christ Jesus my Lord. For his sake I have suffered the loss of all things." The second "I regard" governs the rest of the sentence, all the way to the end of verse 11. The flow of the sentence from that point is: "I consider everything trash, in order that I might gain Christ and in order that I might be found in him, not having my own righteousness . . . but the righteousness from faith, in order to know him, . . . being conformed to his death so as to attain the resurrection" (AT). The syntax of the aorist infinitive "to know" at the beginning of verse 10 is not clear, but it is probably meant to stand in apposition to the two aorist subjunctives, to "gain Christ" and to "be found in him" at the end of verse 8 and beginning of verse 9.

◊ ◊ ◊ ◊

The transition from the previous passage to this one is bridged by Paul's statement in verse 4a and restatement in verse 4b of the same point, put in slightly different ways. Looking back to those who put their confidence in ritual practice, he adds himself to the group, then says that in fact he could *lead* this group because his credentials are superior. He was not a latecomer or convert, but born into Israel and circumcised on the correct day, seven days after birth, or eight counting the day of birth, the ancient way of counting (Gen 17:12; Lev 12:3).

Following this most important credential, Paul asserts his identity by means of three statements: he is of the stock of Israel, the tribe of Benjamin, a Hebrew of the Hebrews. The translation "people" of Israel is inexact for Paul's choice of words, *ek genous Israel*. Proselytes also belonged to the people of Israel, but Paul's emphasis here is that he was born of an Israelite family, so that even by bloodlines he can stake his claim (O'Brien 1991, 370). We know next to nothing else about Paul's family. Acts 23:16-22 suggests that he had relatives in Jerusalem. Jerome in the fourth century reports that Paul's parents were from Gischala (modern Gush Halav) in upper Galilee, taken captive by Romans to Tarsus (*On Illustrious Men 5*). That is certainly plausible, and would explain Paul's Roman citizenship from birth if his father was granted citizenship when he was manumitted, but before the birth of his son, although this is a very late attestation of the tradition.

Paul can also trace his descent from one of the original tribes, something which not many Israelites of his day, other than priests, could probably do. That he was able to do so (also at Rom 11:1) may mean that his family was particularly distinguished or religious. The most illustrious previous member of the tribe of Benjamin was King Saul, for whom its most illustrious first-century member was named in Hebrew, carrying also his Roman name, Paul. Benjamin, a tribe with a small allotment of territory just to the north of that of Judah, was the only tribe that remained loyal to Judah and the Davidic monarchy when the kingdom split after the death of Solomon. Though the territory of Benjamin was small, Jerusalem was located along its southern boundary with Judah. Its loyalty was therefore strategic.

Paul's third qualifying self-description is "Hebrew born of Hebrews," a way of emphasizing his authentic Hebrew origins. Jews tended to speak of themselves not as Jews but as Israelites or Hebrews (see 2 Cor 11:22), though there are some puzzling exceptions (e.g., Gal 2:14-15). Acts 6:1 juxtaposes Hebrews and hellenists in a way that seems to suggest a language distinction between Hebrew or Aramaic-speaking and Greek-speaking Israelites or Jews. But Luke also uses the term "Jews" in pejorative ways to designate those who conspire against Paul (e.g., 23:20; 25:2, 7; 26:2-3 [to a Jewish king!]). If Acts is at all correct about Paul's origins, his own designation of himself as Hebrew here cannot mean Palestinian origins, though it could mean that his first, household language was Hebrew or Aramaic, even in the Diaspora. More likely, though, this self-designation simply means that he has impeccable qualifications from birth to claim all the privileges of membership in Israel.

Paul continues his self-characterization with three phrases that locate him more specifically, with regard to law, zeal, and righteousness. The first, "as to the law, a Pharisee," corroborated by Acts 23:9; 26:5 and perhaps Gal 1:14, places him in that progressive lay (nonpriestly) movement of the intertestamental period about which we know not nearly enough. Gospel portrayals of them as narrow-minded legalists whose main occupation is to conspire against Jesus have long been recognized by scholars as unfair and misleading. Mishnaic and Talmudic references all come later but probably preserve some of their original traditions and sayings. They were the leading Jewish theologians of their day, who attempted to integrate written and oral traditions into a systematic way of life that could provide meaning in changing situations. It was his training as a Pharisee that enabled Paul to come up with new and creative ways of situating the mystery of Christ within a Jewish context of universal salvation.

"As to zeal, a persecutor of the church," Paul's next self-description, is not a contradiction of his Pharisaic identity but a consequence of it. Acts 7:58; 8:1, 3; 9:1-2 describe some of this activity. Because he was extraordinarily eager to propagate religious faith and observance, he took on the extra duty of trying to track down and eliminate those he had considered a threat to that faith and observance. This admission that he persecuted the church is not the regretful lament that it is in 1 Cor 15:9, but a confident assertion that demonstrates his former zeal as a Pharisee—remember that he is trying to impress his readers with how much a Hebrew he really is. That as a Pharisee he would have gone so far in enforcement of his belief is meant to impress. The statement is folded between two assertions about Paul's adherence to the law, and this middle statement is not a digression from that topic but an affirmation of how zealous Paul was for the law.

The third phrase of this triad of self-qualification focuses again on law, though for the sake of literary variation a different term is used, *dikaiosynē,* a very difficult word to translate in English because it covers at least three distinct English semantic areas. A basic meaning is "justice," the doing right that produces the quality of life demanded by life in the covenant community. In biblical contexts outside of Paul's writings it is usually translated "righteousness," for example, in Gen 15:6 LXX, a passage that Paul uses for his own arguments (Rom 4:3; Gal 3:6). But righteousness as a quality inherent in a person, as is intended in Gen 15:6, does not convey the passive sense that Paul intends in his own theology. There, "justification" is the better translation, for it is not our inherent goodness, but quite the contrary, the gift of God in Christ, that mitigates God's wrath and enables us to relate in a familial way to God. It is what God has done, not what we have done. Yet here Paul is not talking about that transformation in Christ, but about his own acceptable status with God based on his previous adherence to the law, and so, his own righteousness, which will later be held in contrast to that new justification of God in verse 9. For the Jew, loving observance of the law is what

89

creates and preserves the bonds of communication with God. Inasmuch as the law could do this, Paul says that he was flawless.

At this point both the topic and the prose change decisively as Paul, after establishing his own strong qualifications to say what he is about to say, presents himself as another example to the Philippians of one who, like Christ Jesus, was willing to relinquish advantage and privilege. He begins to speak of the consequences of the change brought about in him. It is customary to speak of this change as Paul's conversion, but that term may be misleading because of our own connotations. It was not a change from one religion to another, for Paul never saw himself as stepping outside of his membership in Israel or its faith, only extending it in a new direction. Nor was this a change from sinfulness to grace, for he has just said that he was a conscientious observer of his religious obligations, even going well beyond what was required (3:6). If we can speak of a conversion, it is in the realm of a change of orientation, an intellectual and spiritual conversion. From focus on fulfillment of the law, Paul turns to focus on the fulfillment of promise in Jesus the Messiah.

This change of orientation was not a deliberate choice on Paul's part, but was forced on him by his experience of encounter with the Risen Christ. Whether it happened in the dramatic way on the road to Damascus as narrated by Luke (Acts 9, 22, 26), or whether it happened in some way with less fanfare, nevertheless Paul did believe that he had met Christ, or as he put it, God chose to reveal the Son in him (Gal 1:12, 15-16). Paul's way of speaking of this experience emphasizes not his active participation but the action of God in him. The narration of being caught up to the third heaven in 2 Cor 12:1-5 probably describes another different experience. In both cases, we could speak of mystical experiences, understanding "mystical" as a heightened level of awareness and experience of union with God that in no way encourages flight from the world or denial of its reality, but rather plunges the recipient back into the world and its history with a new energy.

Any such encounter with the supernatural necessarily brings about radical changes in the rest of life. Paul's experience was no exception. Verses 7-8 tell us something of what those changes were for him. They consisted basically in a reversal of objects of value and the content of honor. What was gain became loss, and in fact, everything became loss. The language of gain and loss necessarily evokes the background image of balancing the business ledger. Paul is using the rhetorical antitheses of gain and loss and the "all or nothing" approach of verse 8 for literary effect, yet this is not empty rhetoric. He is talking about his own experience. We can only guess about what was previously "gain" that has now become "loss": reputation, privilege, status, self-assurance, and confidence in his own correctness—everything that would constitute the content of his claims to personal honor. One author suggests possible confiscation of property and disinheritance (O'Brien 1991, 389). Another speculates that the loss may have included his wife and children, since it is most likely that Paul had previously been married, but is not at the time he wrote 1 Cor 7, where he expresses a preference for remaining single (Witherington 1994, 93; see further comment on Paul's marital status at 4:3 below).

Verse 8 restates and expands the initial assertion of verse 7 with further very strong rhetorical exaggeration. Now it is not only what was gain that has become loss, but everything must be considered loss in comparison to gaining Christ. Because of him, everything must be surrendered and counted not only as loss, but as *skybala*, rubbish, trash, or yet stronger words to that effect, including excrement: everything that is thrown out in a living situation without plumbing. Both active and passive action are expressed. Paul himself has changed his value system so that everything is loss for the sake of gaining Christ, but this is the result of his having been acted upon by God who in the encounter with Christ has deprived him of everything that was previously an advantage. The verb *ezēmiōthēn* in the aorist passive, here translated "I have suffered," can also mean in business terms "to be fined." In keeping with the ledger terms "loss" and "gain," here Paul says metaphorically that he has received a heavy fine, the loss of everything.

There is a purpose or an exchange for all this loss: to know Christ (vv. 8, 10), to gain him (v. 8), or to be found in him (v. 9).

This language expresses the lived-out continuation of the mystical encounter to which Paul has just referred. The one object of Paul's desires continues to be Christ and whatever Christ wants for him. He now rejects any claim to his own worth or to a self-satisfaction from his own keeping of the law as he did previously (v. 6). Now the basis for any worth or honor comes solely from Christ, whom Paul can only approach through faith. Here as elsewhere, in order to stress the overwhelming goodness that he has found in Christ, he seems to suggest that there is no goodness in the law and that it is bound up only with self-righteousness. We need to remember that it is Paul's stress on the advantage of Christ that makes him speak like this. This is a caricature of what the law means for a faithful law-observant Jew. Elsewhere in other contexts, Paul will also affirm the goodness of the law as part of God's covenant (Rom 7:7-25). The question is not "What is wrong with the law?" but "What is wrong with Paul's former perception of the law?" (Koperski 1992, 236).

In verse 8 Paul refers to knowledge of Christ (rendered as a participle "knowing" in the NRSV) and in verse 10 he uses the infinitive "to know" Christ. Similar expressions occur at 1 Cor 2:2; 2 Cor 5:16, but they are not Paul's usual way of speaking of his relationship to Christ. Much more often, as in verses 9a, 14, he speaks of being "in Christ" as in a corporate body or membership, to such an extent that one can argue that ordinarily Paul did not speak as if he had a personal relationship with Christ, but saw himself as incorporated or embedded in the spiritual existence that is the presence of the Risen Christ in the church. One scholar, Ernst Lohmeyer, proposed that the "knowledge of Christ" here means martyrdom, but that has not been widely accepted, though it could certainly *include* the possibility of martyrdom. Because of the appearance of the word *gnōsis* (knowledge), connections to Gnosticism and the mystical writings of the Hermetic tradition have also been examined, but nothing like this has been made to stick. Given the popularity of some of these expressions with later Gnostics, if there is Gnostic influence, it is the other way around, for example, the influence of Paul's language on Gnosticism and not vice versa (Koperski 1992, 64-65).

Another difficult expression occurs in verse 9: Paul wants his righteousness to be not from the law but from faith in Christ (see NRSV note: or "through the faith of Christ"). Therein lies the ambiguity. The expression *pistis Christou* occurs also in Gal 2:16 and implicitly again in verse 20; 3:22; Rom 3:22, 26 in contexts very similar to the one here. The question is whether in some or all of these cases the genitive is not objective (faith in Christ) but subjective (the faith or fidelity of Christ). The issue has been debated endlessly. While there are in some cases good arguments for the subjective genitive, that interpretation must be rejected here. Paul does not in any other way subjectify or psychologize Christ as does, for instance, Heb 5:7-8. His focus objectifies Christ, remaining on what Christ has done for us and what is our response. (For a good summary of the issues, see Fee 1995, 325.)

Verse 10 begins with Paul's expressed desire to know Christ, repeated from verse 8. The order of objects is Christ himself, then the power *(dynamis)* of his resurrection, then the sharing *(koinōnia)* of his sufferings. The key words "resurrection" and "suffering" are introduced by the two equally significant terms, *dynamis* and *koinōnia*. We have had occasion previously to note the significance of the *koinōnia* word group for Paul's rather unique relationship with the Philippian community. Here it extends beyond horizontal human relationships to communion with Christ. *Dynamis* is also a significant word for Paul. In this letter it appears only here, though the verb, attributed to Christ, will also appear at 3:21. But in other letters, it is clear that all that is accomplished in Christ is done through the power of God; the raising of Christ is the ultimate and most important demonstration of that power, which makes Christ himself the manifestation of God's power (cf. Rom 1:4; 15:13, 19; 1 Cor 1:18, 24; 5:4; 6:14; 2 Cor 4:7; 12:9).

Paul's entrance into sharing in the resurrection is through suffering, not just for its own sake, but after the example of Christ, "by becoming like him in his death," really by being joined to the form, or conforming, to his death *(symmorphizomenos)*. Just as Christ did not cling to the form *(morphē)* of God, but changed it and took that of a slave (2:6, 7), so Paul wishes to change his form to that of the death of Christ. This statement more than anything else in the passage suggests the anticipation of martyrdom, and this could likely be part of the intent, but it is not that simple. Paul's reflection is not primarily future oriented, but past and present. The suffering whereby he has lost everything (3:8) is already part of that dying, as is his present suffering in prison. It is a lifelong process begun with Paul's initial encounter with the Risen Christ, and will be completed at his actual death.

One wonders about the order—resurrection, then suffering. Paul is not thinking here in chronological order, but rather he places first the overwhelming mystery in which he is taken up, the reality that the one he encountered had been raised from the dead by God. Then, just as he had used the *koinōnia* word group earlier in the letter to describe his relationship with the Philippian community and their relationship in the Spirit, and will do so again later (Phil 1:5; 2:1; 4:15), here he uses the same expression to speak of his (and implicitly their) sharing in the suffering of Christ. Everything is by participation in Christ and in the Spirit: union, exaltation, and suffering.

It must be noted, however, that verses 10-11 form an inclusion in which the two outer terms are "the resurrection" and the inner ones are "suffering" and "death," so that when the two verses are taken together as the conclusion of the very long sentence that began at the beginning of verse 8, the order in this concluding part of the sentence is really resurrection-suffering-death-resurrection. Thus suffering and death are enfolded within the grounding mystery of the resurrection of Christ, expanded in its final appearance at the end of verse 11 to its soteriological referent, the resurrection of the faithful dead in the footsteps of Christ.

It is quite clear in 1 Cor 15, the gem of Paul's teaching on resurrection, that for him the raising of Christ from the dead does not make much sense unless it is the beginning of a larger process that includes *our* resurrection. The hellenistic world was full of dying and rising gods and semi-gods. With the idea of Christ being raised from the dead, the Gentile Corinthians would have had no problem. Their problem was, rather, Paul's insistence on extending that belief to us. But within the framework of Jewish apocalyptic theology, the emphasis is on the resurrection of at least the just, if not all (beliefs about the universality of resurrection varied). Here in Philippians, both beliefs come together beautifully. Through the power of Christ's resurrection, attained only through suffering and death, we too can be brought into the same mystery. Verses 10-11 are a small recap of 2:6-11 with the addition of the sequel that regards us: We too share in the resurrection.

Yet both in Greek and in translation, verse 11 sounds not sure and confident, but conditional and hopeful. Why does Paul not state more boldly, as he does in 1 Cor 15, that resurrection is also our destiny? The answer lies in the autobiographical nature of the passage and therefore the requisite modesty of expression. As will become clear in the next verses, he recognizes that he is on the way but not yet arrived. He hopes, but does not know for certain, that he will be able to endure to the end (see Otto 1995). The uncertainty expressed in the statement is not about the future resurrection but about his own fidelity.

We see in this passage one of the most beautiful expressions of Paul's life in Christ, and indeed one of the most profound formulations of the mystery of Christ in the entire New Testament. It is the earliest Christian conversion story, taking into account the warnings expressed above about various understandings of conversion. In this passage Paul looks back after a period of years spent in missionary activity to reflect on the impact made on him by his encounter with the Risen Christ. While Acts describes it in dramatic terms drawn from traditional theophany symbolism (bright light, blindness, a heavenly voice), Paul speaks in much simpler terms, not of how it happened but of what changes it has produced in him. It has made him a person with a single passion: to maintain and strengthen the relationship with Christ begun years earlier, but not in an isolated individualist or narcissistic way. Always for Paul, being in Christ means being in community, which is the body of Christ expressing his presence in the world.

Conformity to Christ, a key idea in the latter part of this passage, is conformity to suffering and death in order to be conformed to resurrection. Paul had an uncanny way, so early in the Christian tradition, of seeing an intimate connection between the fate of Jesus and the life of Christians. Only about twenty-five years after the crucifixion of Jesus, when the memory was still fresh, witnesses were still alive, and crucifixion was frequently practiced, Paul could find meaning in that awful fate. If we compare the conformity of Jesus to the human condition in 2:6, 7 with the conformity of Paul, and by implication of all believers, to the condition of Jesus in 3:10-11, we have an early formulation of what was later to become a key idea about the work of grace in the Incarnation and the Christian life: that the entry of divinity into our humanity was for the sake of gradually but surely transforming humanity into divine life.

RUNNING THE RACE FOR THE HEAVENLY PRIZE (3:12-16)

The same conversation continues. Verse 12 is built on the structure, "not that . . . , nor that . . . but. . . ." It is not that Paul has already received or obtained what he has so longingly described in the preceding verses, nor is it the case that he has "already reached the goal" or been perfected. The second verb *teteleiōmai,* like its related noun *telos* and adjective *teleios,* carries the twofold and somewhat distinct meanings of end or goal, and completion or fulfillment. Perhaps the most difficult use of the word group, which has inspired generations of frustration, occurs in Matt 5:48, where the listeners are told to be *teleioi* as their heavenly Father is *teleios.* Perfect? Fulfilled? Complete? Mature? Whatever it is supposed to be that both we and God can be boggles the mind. Here at 3:12, probably the best understanding is something akin to attaining the goal in view, especially since the metaphor of the footrace will be invoked in the next verses. The adjective will reappear in verse 15 with a meaning closer to that in Matt 5:48 (see also Matt 19:21). Paul is clear that he is still involved in an ongoing process. He may also want to stress that the resurrection is a future event that has not already been fulfilled, as some in the church seemed to believe (2 Tim 2:18), and as can be construed from some passages in John's Gospel and the later Pauline letters (e.g., John 5:24-25; 11:25-26; Col 3:1).

Verses 12-13 contain four different tenses of the verb *lambanein*, "to receive," and its compound, *katalambanein*, "to seize or comprehend," in both meanings of that English word: to enclose and to understand. The variants on meaning are played upon in the ways in which it is used. In the NRSV, the first, simple aorist, *elabon* from the verb *lambanō*, is translated "obtained," while the others of the compound verb *katalambanō* in the aorist subjunctive, aorist passive, and perfect infinitive are translated "make one's own." This consistent translation of the compound verb and its close similarity to the meaning of the original verb preserve the use of the common verb in the Greek. Familiarity with the Greek text also allows us to recognize that in verse 12 and the beginning of verse 13, listeners are in fact hearing multiple repetitions of the same verb. Thus the second half of verse 12 contains a neat play on active and passive voices of the same verb, *katalambanein*. The NRSV translation renders the twist: "I press on to make it my own, because Christ Jesus has made me his own." A more literal translation would show the turn of phrase even better: "I press on if I might also take hold, inasmuch as I also have been taken hold of by Christ Jesus."

Another interesting verb in these verses is the third one in verse 12 and the first in verse 14: "I press on" *(diōkō)*. The same verb has another meaning pertinent to Paul: "to persecute," which he has used with himself as subject, "persecutor of the church," in verse 6 (also 1 Cor 15:9). Here, he pursues the goal, the risen life in Christ Jesus, in similar fashion to the way he once pursued believers in that same Christ from a good conscience, believing that he was doing the will of God and following the law. The difficult connector, *eph' hō*, can mean "because" or "inasmuch as" or "for which," or several other meanings in different contexts. Its ambiguity has caused considerable difficulty and misunderstanding in Rom 5:12 as to Paul's intent about the relationship of

Adam's sin to ours and to the universal sentence of death. There it is best understood as "because" or "inasmuch as." Here a closer connection may be implied. It is not only because Christ has taken hold of Paul that he presses on toward the goal of resurrection, but since he is conformed to Christ's death (v. 10), there is a transforming process at work, and a dynamic relationship between Paul's being taken hold of, which is prior, and his taking hold. He is speaking of the passive and active aspects of his experience of being in Christ. He adds in verse 13a that he realizes he has not yet attained the goal, which still lies ahead.

The future orientation comes to the fore in verses 13-14, where Paul says that he has made it a habit to let go of what has passed, his former life and its values, in order to embrace a new identity that now impels him forward. In this whole passage, Paul is proposing himself as a model (clear in v. 17), so there is a subtle hint here that the Philippians can do the same with their community problems. Here the imagery of the footrace begins. Paul throws off anything that would hold him back, and runs for the end line and the prize (cf. use of the footrace metaphor extended to everyone in 1 Cor 9:24-25 and Heb 12:1-2). The prize is the "calling up," which probably has two levels of meaning. The first continues the metaphor of the footrace and represents the moment at which the victorious athlete is called forward to receive the prize (O'Brien 1991, 431-32). But it is also interpreted correctly as the "heavenly call" in the NRSV, for heaven was of course thought to be above, where Christ was seated at the right hand of God (Pss 3:1; 110:1) and could, to continue the metaphor, award the best prize: eternal life. This call was continuous with the call addressed to each believer at conversion, to which Paul and other New Testament writers often allude (e.g., 1 Cor 1:24, 27; 7:20; 2 Thess 1:11; 2 Pet 1:10). As community, they are called to be the holy ones (Rom 1:7; 1 Cor 1:2). Here the same image is extended into the eschatological realm.

Everything Paul has been saying from verse 4 on, even though said in the first-person singular, has been for the purpose of proposing himself as an example of one who is willing to lose a great deal in order to gain Christ, with the hope that the

Philippians who are causing dissension will take the hint and do likewise. At verses 15-16, he turns from first-person singular to the hortatory first-person plural to bring his hearers directly into the argument. He addresses those who are like himself *teleoi* (see discussion of the word group above at v. 12), here appropriately translated by the NRSV as "mature." There is a certain tension between the use of this word in verse 12 and here in verse 15, since in verse 12 Paul has said that he has *not* reached the end of the process, whereas here it seems to suggest that some, including himself, have. The solution is in different nuances of the same word group. Here at verse 15 the meaning is close to that in Matt 5:48; 19:21 (see also 1 Cor 2:6; 14:20; Eph 4:13; Col 1:28), maturity or fulfillment consonant with one's state and phase of life. There is no need to suppose that Paul has in mind a select group in Philippi, especially those who think of themselves as "perfect" over against others, as is sometimes proposed. After all, he includes himself. "Those of us . . . who" is a rhetorical device intended to motivate all hearers to want to be included.

The rest of verse 15 returns to language used at 1:7; 2:2, 5 introducing the hymn of chapter 2: the verb *phronein,* to have an attitude or orientation in thinking (also at 3:19; 4:10). The same language will be used for the problem of Euodia and Syntyche in 4:2. Those who think differently from the path Paul has just laid out are promised/threatened that God will set them straight. But how? The language is loaded: God will reveal *(apokalypsei)* it all to you. The verb and its related noun are often connected in the Pauline letters with eschatological revelation (Rom 1:17-18; 2:5; 8:19; 1 Cor 2:10), the return of Christ (1 Cor 1:7; 2 Thess 1:7), or even an earth-shaking appearance to persons, including Paul himself (Gal 1:16; 2:2). But they can also have a less spectacular meaning when he is speaking of spiritual gifts (1 Cor 14:6, 26), a special insight or message from God communicated during the prayer assembly. Perhaps this is closer to the meaning here. Paul hopes that through prayer and the right kind of community pressure, all will come to agree with him. The moderately coercive tone that comes through is no doubt intended. The primary goal is to persuade his hearers to come around to his point of view.

Verse 16 pleads with them by expressing the hope that all will keep going in the direction to which they have so far arrived. The first verb, *phthanein,* translated "hold fast" in the NRSV, often means to go before, but here has the more general meaning of arriving at a certain point. The second, *stoichein,* is more ambiguous and is not reflected well in the NRSV translation, "what we have attained." It can mean to stand firm or to proceed along a preestablished line (Acts 21:24; Rom 4:12; Gal 5:25; 6:16), perhaps even to march together; thus figuratively, to agree, as here. The sense of the whole statement is encouragement to keep from both backsliding and stagnating: "We have come this far; let's keep going."

THE HOPE OF TRANSFORMATION THROUGH EXAMPLE (3:17–4:1)

For the fourth time in the letter, Paul addresses his hearers with the familial title "brothers" (1:12; 3:1, 13; another yet to come at 4:1), a common form of address (with "sisters") in the Pauline communities. We are justified in translating "brothers and sisters," since it is clear in other contexts, and especially here soon at 4:2, that Paul does not intend to exclude women. The common public forms of address did not acknowledge the presence of women, who were to be socially invisible in public situations. He asks that the Philippians be "co-imitators," *summimētai* of him or with him. The simple noun *mimētēs* is common, but this compound form appears nowhere else.

Paul is summarizing and concluding the appeal that he has been making throughout the chapter: to take himself as an example of how to let go of what seemed essential for the sake of a greater good, just as he had previously presented Christ in the same light in chapter 2. This is not the only time that he has posed himself and others as model (1 Cor 4:16; 1 Thess 1:6; 2 Thess 3:7, 9; Eph 5:1 escalates to imitation of God). The question is often raised of how putting oneself forward for imitation is consonant with Christian humility. That is not really the issue, however. Paul is a public figure, a founding apostle, and an authority. The master-disciple model necessitates this kind of relationship between leader and followers. The key is 1 Cor 11:1, another passage in which he is trying to convince the hearers that they can relinquish some of their own will for the good of the whole. There Paul says, in effect, "Imitate me as I imitate Christ." What is said in 3:1 is shorthand for that full statement, and that should already be apparent from everything he has said in 3:7-11. Paul never poses himself as an end but rather as a means to Christ. He has just been trying to drive home a specific point about allowing loss of status and privilege for the sake of others. They cannot reproach him with "Practice what you preach."

There is a further question about the use of the compound, "co-imitate." With whom does he envision himself to be? The NRSV's "join in imitating me" is one way to understand it; Paul bids them come together in their learning from his example. Another approach is suggested by the rest of the sentence, in which he associates himself with others who have walked in the same path as he, so as to become a "type" or imprint set before their eyes. Here he must surely mean Timothy and Epaphroditus as well as others known to the Philippians as star examples of what Christian lives should be. They are to consider well, to survey or contemplate *(skopein)* those who "walk" *(peripatein)* according to the example given by Paul and others associated with him. Another word meaning "progress in the way already begun" is added to that already discussed in verse 16.

Verses 18-19 return to the dark side, briefly recalling 1:15-17 and 3:2. The purpose of these brief asides is to propose two alternatives, the right and the wrong, and thus strengthen the sense of in-group by heightening the contrast between the two. Here the issue is different from 1:15-17, where the reproach was to those who preach the authentic gospel but from unworthy motives. Those in 3:2 do not, according to Paul, preach the authentic gospel at all. That same issue may be at stake here. It is difficult to know who within the circle of Christ-believers could be so inimical to the cross of Christ and what their belly has to do with it. For this opposition to the Cross we must go to Galatians, where Paul warns of the scandal or stumbling block of the Cross as alternative to circumcision, even as occasion of persecution for those who give up circumcision (Gal 5:11; 6:12). He poses the symbol of the Cross as direct opposition to those who would go the way of belief in Christ through the mediation of the Mosaic law. The letter to the Galatians is peppered with references to the Cross and its role in Paul's and the Christian's life, more so than any other Pauline letter (besides those mentioned, 3:1; 5:24; 6:14).

Probably these "enemies of the cross of Christ" are those who preach circumcision rather than the scandal (to Jewish hearers) of a law-free gospel based on the crucifixion and resurrection of Christ. Then the reference is to the same group as in 3:2, and as argued there, not a group represented in Philippi, but used as a foil in contrast to what will come in verse 20. In contrast to the expectation of a savior (v. 20), they are headed for destruction. In contrast to the heavenly destiny of Paul's believers, they are focused on earthly things. Once again here Paul uses the important verb *phronein:* they have their minds and attitudes set not on the good things from above but on what is of the earth in contrast to heaven. Verse 19 contains four statements in inclusive structure. The first and fourth are roughly synonymous: destruction is the destiny of those whose attention is on earthly rather than heavenly things. The second and third terms are also very closely related, if not synonymous.

Most commentators see one of two possibilities for these belly-worshipers: either they are libertines beset by gluttony and lust who have abused the Pauline doctrine of freedom, or they are people obsessed with circumcision, food laws, and other fine points of the law that Paul sees as oppressive rather than liberating. If the circumcision group is intended, Paul is badly caricaturing law observers for rhetorical effect. This "belly" that they are obsessed with is *koilia,* a term for the inner parts of the lower body: stomach, intestines, and womb. Here it would have to be construed as a euphemism for the sexual organs, with a similar meaning in its correlate statement that paradoxically contrasts honor and shame (see 1 Cor 12:23). One problem with this interpretation is that while there is of course a close connection between the social concept of shame and *abuse* of sex, there is no good evidence that links the notion of shame to the male sexual organs as such, which would be the case here with a reference to circumcision. On the contrary, the male sexual organs are seen as a major locus of pride and honor. If the "libertine" interpretation is followed, their shame could be not objectified in the sexual organs but is used as a reference to their shameful behavior.

The one major problem with the circumcision interpretation is Rom 16:17-18, where Paul also refers to those who serve their *koilia* instead of Christ, but these opponents are not explicitly preachers of circumcision. Rather, they are creators of dissent and deceit, which might suggest people like those in Philippi who are causing the dissension there. However, in this passage in Romans it is never said what is the source of dissension. A reading of Rom 14–15 suggests that the dissension is in fact over table sharing and food observances (cf. Rom 14:2). The objection that Rom 16:17-18 suggests an issue other than circumcision may therefore be groundless, because food-law issues would inevitably have been tied to the circumcision issue. Probably the best interpretation of these objectionable people in Philippians is that this is another reference to the circumcision party who have already been pilloried at 3:2.

Verses 20-21 change tone abruptly, in deliberate contrast to the preceding verses. From verse 17 forward, Paul is saying, "Follow my example, not that of those people, our enemies, and look what good things are coming." Verse 20 is charged with two important political terms: *politeuma* (citizenship or commonwealth) and *sōtēr* (savior). A *politeuma* was a self-governing group with specific rights and voting procedures within a city, or other kinds of groups constructed along these lines, for example, professional or burial clubs, festal associations of women, associations of soldiers originating from the same place, or a group of citizens of a city living together in another place (Lüderitz 1994), such as the Jewish community of Alexandria (*Ant.* 12.2.108, though what kind of civic rights the Alexandrian Jews had is much disputed). This last meaning, a culturally or religiously identifiable group living somewhere other than their place of provenance, is closest to the way Paul uses it. Figuratively, believers are citizens of another, heavenly city, where their true citizenship lies. Here on earth, therefore, they are transients who do not really belong.

The idea of the heavenly destiny of Christians is pervasive in early Christianity, though Paul is the first to put it in writing. Other New Testament writers express the same idea by use of the word groups related to the terms *paroikos* (Eph 2:19; Heb 11:9; 1 Pet 1:7; 2:11) and *parepidēmos* (Heb 11:13; 1 Pet 1:1; 2:11), both with a similar meaning (even though 1 Pet 2:11 uses them in apposition). Originally meaning one who lives alongside something, both words acquired the meaning of sojourner, stranger, and thus noncitizen. These terms are not used in Philippians, but the same idea is rendered positively by the idea that the place where Christians really are citizens is not here. The hearers had already been reminded of this at 1:27 (see comment there), where they were exhorted to conduct themselves as citizens who meet the requirements of their own citizenship, as specified in the proclamation of Christ.

The potential tension that this idea and the lived experience behind it could cause in everyday life is discussed using the same image in an early second-century Roman text, the *Shepherd of Hermas* (*Similitude* 1). The focus there is on the crisis that will be caused from having too many possessions. Hearers are told that they are living in a city not their own, but that they really belong to another city with its own laws and king. If they get too invested in this city where they are sojourning, what will they do when the ruler of this city says, "Either follow my law or get out"? Will they cling to their possessions and because of them deny their own city and its law in favor of this foreign city in which they have so much invested? This ancient version of "You can't take it with you" is precisely the kind of conflict that could be stirred up when the going got tough, and which in those circumstances became the stuff of apostasy or martyrdom. Recall the heavily Roman influence in Philippi and the presence of large numbers of Roman citizens, and this affirmation could be heard as directly anti-imperial. Given the oblique allusion to suffering in 1:29, we may have grounds to think not that there was open persecution of Christians in Philippi, but that some were experiencing ostracism and social rejection of various kinds because of their beliefs. In the second century another early Christian writer speaks of Christians living in all cities and countries, none of which is their own (*Ep. Diog.* 5-6).

The naming of a savior from this true heavenly city of Christians is no less a political statement. In the Hebrew Scriptures, a *goel* is one who redeems ancestral land, or who ransoms or in some other way rescues persons who are in trouble or who are alienated. He does this because he is bound through kinship or other social ties to protect them. Understandably, the term became widely used of God, especially in the Exodus event (e.g., Exod 6:6; 15:15; Ps 74:2; Prov 23:11; Isa 51:10; Jer 50:34). The Greek title, assumed for centuries by hellenistic rulers, was also given to various gods, especially the healing god Asclepius, and to military victors. It referred not to an eschatological figure, but to someone powerful enough to bring stability and protection to a population in the here and now. As one author puts it, since the Battle of Actium in 31 BCE, the Philippians already had a lord and savior, Octavian Augustus, who had assumed sole power in the Roman world, and to whom the title was frequently ascribed. The close association of the two terms *politeuma* and *sōtēr* could not help having political connotations alternative to Roman loyalty. Just as Philippi was a colony of Rome and every Philippian's allegiance should be to Caesar, so the church was a colony of heaven and its allegiance went there (Fee 1995, 379).

This is the only place in the authentic Pauline letters where Christ is called "savior" (also in Eph 5:23; 2 Tim 1:10; Titus 1:4; 2:13). Did Paul generally avoid the term because of its political connotations, and deliberately use it here for the same reason? The savior that Christians expect comes from their true home, heaven, not from anywhere on earth. Most human savior figures in the Greek world were hailed with the title because of what they had already done, a pledge of future performance, and the redemptive death of Jesus is certainly in the background here. But

Paul throws the entire emphasis on the future. The verb "expect" *(apekdechomai)* "always focuses on what is definite, future, and eschatological" (O'Brien 1991, 462). Its other famous location in Paul's letters is Rom 8, where it indicates what all of creation as well as believers do while waiting for God's revelation of what is to come (8:19, 23, 25).

The salvation expected and hoped for is of the nature of transformation of human existence in resurrection (v. 21), which Paul has already spoken about in his own case in 3:10-11. Here he generalizes the same hope to all. Just as Christ Jesus took on the form or shape *(schēma)* of humanity (2:7), so too he will change *(metaschēmatizein)* our humanity in the opposite direction through the glory of resurrection. Elsewhere Paul has used this verb only once with a neutral and weak meaning (1 Cor 4:6), and in one other context with quite negative meaning: the transformation that Satan and his followers can accomplish to deceive (2 Cor 11:13-15). Here the import is totally other. Just as Christ took on the form *(morphē)* of a slave (2:7), so he will join our humanity to make it conformable *(symmorphon)* to his glory.

The contrast is between "the body of our humiliation," not a very comprehensible translation in the NRSV but a good literal one, and "the body of his glory." Better translations, as suggested in the notes, would be "our humble bodies" and "his glorious body." But the more literal translations preserve the paradoxical contrast. Body to body, the lowering of Christ to meet us results in our exaltation. While resurrection belief tends to focus on physical transformation, the Greek word rendered body *(sōma)* has many levels of meaning and cannot be limited to the physical aspect of persons as opposed to the spiritual aspect. It is the means by which we can perceive the presence of a person, which includes not only perceptible matter but also aspects of personhood and personality. The *sōma* is the person.

Though the word *resurrection* is never used in this passage, that is what it is all about. Transformation and glorification are seen by Paul only in that context. Remember too that he cannot consider the resurrection of Jesus without the context of resurrection as the destiny of all the faithful. The only difference is that it has happened to Jesus first. The rest of the process will be accomplished by God through the cosmic power given by God to Jesus in his resurrection. The source of this idea, or at least one of its most effective drivers, is Ps 110:1, an enthronement hymn for a royal coronation, understood messianically by Christians to be said about God addressing Christ: "The LORD says to my lord, 'Sit at my right hand until I make your enemies your footstool,' " or put them under your feet. We can see the echoes of that verse, along with Dan 7:14, throughout the New Testament as the prophetic prediction of Christ's enthronement in the resurrection (e.g., Matt 26:64; 28:18; Mark 14:62; Luke 22:69; Acts 2:33; 5:31; 7:55; Rom 8:34; Eph 1:20; Col 3:1; Heb 1:3; 1 Pet 3:22; Rev 5:1, and others). Here in Philippians the emphasis is not on Christ's position at the throne of God, but on the authority given him to subject all opposition (also 1 Cor 15:25-28). In 1 Cor 15, Paul connects the triumph of Christ especially with his victory over death: "The last enemy to be destroyed is death" (v. 26). That is what his resurrection accomplishes for all believers.

Verse 4:1 is the conclusion to the previous topic and at the same time forms a transition to the next. The language with which Paul addresses the Philippians in this verse is probably the most affectionate that he uses with any community to which his letters have been preserved. This is the language of the literary tradition of friendship. Along with other lines in the same vein such as 1:7-8, 25-26, it is what prompts commentators to classify the letter's genre that way (see further discussion in the introduction). They are his beloved (*agapētoi*, also at 2:12 and elsewhere in the Pauline letters). This affectionate title is stressed by being affirmed at both the beginning and the end of verse 1. (The NRSV translation, "whom I love and long for . . . my beloved" sounds as if the first reference is a verb and the second a noun, but in Greek both are the same noun, forming a circle around the rest of the sentence.) They are also those he longs for (*epipothētoi*, the only time he calls a community by this title), his joy, another mention of this pervasive theme in the letter, and his crown. A figurative reference to a crown or wreath in the literature of this period is ordinarily a reward for struggle, based on the image of the prize of a wreath made of various natural components awarded to the winner in an athletic competition (1 Cor 9:25; 2 Tim 4:8; Jas 1:12; 1 Pet 5:4; Rev 2:10). It is an unusual way to refer to a group of persons (but also at 1 Thess 2:19). The question is therefore to be raised whether this usage bears a future, eschatological implication. But that is not necessary. Just as Paul calls the Corinthians the result of his work and the seal of his apostleship (1 Cor 9:1-2), so here the athletic metaphor is employed. The Philippians are the proof that he is running the race well.

Paul has used several verbs of position in his exhortation to the Philippians to be all that he wants them to be: conduct themselves as citizens (*politeuesthai*, 1:27), walk or proceed (*peripatein*, 3:17), and stand firm (*stēkein*, 1:27). The last one is again used in 4:1 to draw together the whole discussion, especially the contrast of the preceding verses. They are not to be like the negative example of verses 18-19, but like those who expect their savior from their true home. In that faith and hope they are to stand firm without wavering.

This chapter contains some of the most powerful theological lines in the Pauline corpus. As Paul reflects on his own experience with the purpose of inspiring his hearers to imitate his example in their own lives, he reveals the lesson he has learned from discipleship in the particular way in which he has been called to live it. The reversal of the value system that came perhaps gradually but still surely after his encounter with the Risen Christ changed his whole life, even though he remained a loyal member of Israel. Within that identity, his perspective changed radically so that everything previously considered something to be clung to now became loss. On the other side of that loss, however, was incomparable new gain, that of knowing Christ Jesus. Though Paul probably did not compose the hymn of chapter 2, and though it may have been originally composed for an entirely different purpose and with a different Christology in view, Paul's interpretation of it fit perfectly into the framework of his letter, and he was able then to speak of his own experience as a reflection of that of Christ.

The motif of heavenly citizenship expressed at 3:20 could be used as justification for noninvolvement in history and its challenges: If Christians do not really belong here, what is the point of trying to change anything? It must be remembered that Paul's eschatological worldview contributed to a certain detachment rather than involvement, whatever he and his followers actually believed about the return of Christ—and that is not at all clear. At the same time, he is very clear about community obligations and ideals, and does not tolerate abuses in that realm. This is very clear in the various problems about which he comments and gives orders in 1 Corinthians. Even here, the disunity in the church is a source of great dismay to him. Within the limited extent that Christians could change their world toward the values of God, they were expected to do so.

APPEAL TO UNITY AND JOY (4:2-9)

Verses 2-3 are the culmination of the argument for unity that Paul has been making throughout the letter. Here he actually names the two people who are at the heart of the problem. Verses 4-9 move quickly to a very different tone, lighter and full of general parenesis, or moral instruction, that seems not to be directed to any particular problem or issue. These verses, like 3:1, sound as if the writer is coming to a conclusion; in fact, verse 8 again uses the expression that appears there: *to loipon,* which can mean "finally" or "in conclusion" but also "in summary" (of what has just preceded). For those who argue for multiple fragments in the letter, verse 9 is the conclusion of one of the fragments. For those who see a single letter, it is the conclusion of one section before the beginning of a new and final one (see discussion of theories of composition and structure in the introduction).

◊ ◊ ◊ ◊

In verse 2, Paul makes a deliberate and individual appeal in strong language to each of two women, Euodia and Syntyche, whose names could be roughly translated as "good journey" and "good luck." Both names are attested elsewhere in inscriptions. He repeats his verb "I urge Euodia and I urge Syntyche" to agree *(to auto phronein)* in the Lord. The use of this by now familiar verb brings Paul's concern here into the mainstream of his appeal to unity in the whole letter (1:7; 2:2, 5; 3:15, 19; 4:10). The passage has been the subject of much controversy because it gives us such a tantalizing glimpse of something, then bars the shutters. Three questions must be pursued, the answers to all of which were so obvious to the Philippians that they did not need to be mentioned. First, what is the position of these two women in the community? Second, how important is their disagreement to Paul's concerns and the rest of the community? Third, what was the cause of their quarrel?

First, commentators who believe that Euodia and Syntyche occupied important positions in the community frequently allude to purported evidence for the high status of Macedonian women. But most of this evidence has to do with Macedonian queens of the late-classical and hellenistic periods, which has very little if anything to do with ordinary women of the Roman period living in a Roman colony. Another approach is to demonstrate the popularity of women's cults in Philippi, especially those of Artemis/Hecate/Diana, also syncretized with the Thracian goddess Bendis. This material makes interesting background information against which to reconstruct the lives of Philippian women, but probably has little bearing on the customs in force about women's social freedom and leadership.

What can be pointed to, however, is the indication that by the Augustan age, Roman women were enjoying greater social freedom, in spite of apparently continuous oppressive legal restraints, than their foremothers a century before. This may have some bearing on the possibility of women in strong leadership positions. We are reminded of Phoebe in Rom 16:1-2, a *diakonos* of the church of Cenchrae, one of the seaports of Corinth, a Roman commercial colony. Thus we know that in Pauline churches, women could occupy the position of *diakonos*—whatever function such a person fulfilled. Both Rom 16 and other texts point in the direction of official travel or representation of the church to outsiders. John Chrysostom, who was no feminist but was the first on record to acknowledge Junia as an apostle in Rom 16:7, is ambiguous but encouraging by calling Euodia and Syntyche together the *kephalaion* (principal characters) of the Philippian church (*Homily 13 on Philippians,* NPNF First Series 13.244).

Given the opening lines of the letter, we know that there were persons called *diakonoi* in the Philippian church, and the generic masculine plural of the title in 1:1 does not exclude the presence of women among them. Thus Davorin Peterlin, for instance, concludes that Euodia and Syntyche were among their numbers (1995, 106-11). There is another possibility, however. The text of 1:1 gives two kinds of titles: besides *diakonoi* there are also *episkopoi,* mentioned first (see comment on 1:1). We know that the first generations of Christians met largely in private houses under the patronage of the owner of the house (Rom 16:4-5; 1 Cor 16:19). Many would argue that these household patrons became the local pastoral leaders, eventually forming a council of leaders in a certain city or region. We also know that some of these house-church patrons were women, with no mention of their husbands (Acts 12:12; Col 4:15), probably widows with sufficient resources to keep their households running. These two women are called "coworkers" *(synergoi)* by Paul, a title he sometimes gives to fellow itinerant missionaries (e.g., 2:25; 1 Cor 3:9; 1 Thess 3:2) but also to resident leaders, as here (cf. Rom 16:3; Phlm 1; 3 John 8). There is a grammatical possibility that only Clement is intended to be a coworker in that statement, but that is not likely, and hardly any commentator reads it that way. There is also a manuscript variant that would exclude any of those named in the sentence from being Paul's coworkers ("with Clement and my coworkers and the rest . . ." [AT]), but the variant is not accepted by most textual critics. Considering the evidence for women leaders of house-churches, what best fits is that Euodia and Syntyche, important enough to be called "coworkers" by Paul, were in fact *episkopoi,* that is, heads of local house-churches and thus strategic members of the church. Those who hesitate to accept this interpretation may be clinging too strongly to later connotations of the word *episkopos,* which at this time have not yet arisen.

Second, is their quarrel central to Paul's concern for unity, or does it come up here as an afterthought to his earlier appeals? Commentators are divided on this point, even those who analyze the structure of the letter based on ancient rhetorical rules, into two general groups: those who think their disagreement was very important, and those who think it was the central cause of the whole problem. Few contemporary commentators would hold that Paul took the time and effort to single them out in the way he did if this was some petty quarrel that had no repercussions on the whole church. The perception of the average reader is skewed by the chapter division at 4:1, leading to the impression that a new topic is beginning. Remember that Paul did not write the letter in chapters and verses. A more natural division, in fact, comes at 4:4, so that 4:2-3 can be seen as the conclusion to a long section beginning as early as 2:1. The same expression, *to auto phronein,* appears at both 2:2 and 2:4 (subjunctive in 2:2, infinitive in 2:4), and that particular expression is found nowhere else in Philippians (see Rom 12:16; 15:5; 2 Cor 13:11). Thus it seems that the disagreement between Euodia and Syntyche is central to the problem in Philippi, not "just a case of two bickering women" (Furnish 1985, 103), or even just another important topic, but the topic to which all appeals to unity are oriented.

The third question is by far the most difficult, and one to which we will never know the answer: Why did they quarrel? What was the cause and impetus of their division? One line of interpretation suggests that theirs was a contest for honor, credibility, and reputation, that the difficulty was simply a personality clash, a competition for power and authority. They had yet to learn the lesson that Paul was trying to teach in his examples of the emptying of Christ and of his own value system. This makes it into a personal, one-to-one conflict. If we would like to attribute some good sense to them, however, perhaps there is more to it than that. If their dissension did divide the community, there must be some issue involved, and it must involve more than two people. Their influence has produced groups of followers in dissent with one another—and perhaps more than two groups. One possible issue that could be the source of the trouble is the question of circumcision and observances of the law, but the interpretation taken in this commentary is that that is not a real issue in Philippi (see comment on 3:2-3).

Another possibility is that their argument is about Paul, his credibility and his authority, and he is trying to stay impartial. The common assumption is that the two women are in conflict with each other. It is also possible that together they are in conflict with Paul, and that the problem pits some in the community, led by Euodia and Syntyche, against Paul. In this case his appeal to them to be of one mind means to be of one mind *with him* (Kittredge 1996, 142-44). In other letters, however, especially 1 and 2 Corinthians, Paul is quite open about refuting the arguments of those who are against him or think differently than he does. Moreover, as we have seen, this letter is characterized by a particular tone of affection, so a conflict of Philippians against Paul is a less likely scenario.

In verse 3 Paul asks a third party to mediate in the dispute between the two women. The way in which he does it suggests a rather polite but firm approach, unlikely therefore to refer to one of his trusted helpers whom he would assign with less polish. The identity of this third person has been much disputed, and is likely to remain so. Part of the trouble is that the word can either be a proper name or a word with its own meaning. The male name *Syzygos* is possible but not attested as a proper name except in compounds. It is more likely that this is a word literally meaning "yoked together," thus traditionally translated "yokefellow" (RSV) or in more contemporary usage, "companion" (NRSV). If so, to whom the reference referred was obvious to the Philippians but not at all obvious to us. Epaphroditus, the bearer of the letter (2:25), is a likely candidate, since Paul speaks so highly of him and he seems to be from Philippi (2:25-30). Other suggestions have included Barnabas, Luke, Silas, and Timothy (Lightfoot 1982, 158-59).

113

The suggestions have not been limited to men, however. Already Clement of Alexandria in the second century (*Stromata* 3.6.53.1), followed by Origen (*Commentary on Romans* 1.1), began taking seriously the original reference to a yoke embedded in the word, and suggested that the referent was Paul's wife, left behind in Philippi, the community with which he got along best and would therefore presumably feel most comfortable leaving her. Both commentators were, in context, defending the good of marriage and wanted to portray Paul as married, apparently ignoring the good indications that he was not married at the time he wrote 1 Cor 7. Another suggested female has been Lydia, for otherwise, the letter's silence about a key figure in the founding of the Philippian church (according to Acts 16) has always been a conundrum. A reference to her here would argue for her continuing central importance in the community, but still would not explain the absence of a direct reference to her by name. Later, others fancifully combined both suggestions and made Lydia Paul's wife!

The problem word along with its modifier *gnēsios* (true, genuine, but hardly "loyal" as in the NRSV) is in the vocative case, thus *gnēsie syzyge*. Because the vocative of the modifier is masculine in form, distinguished from the feminine form *gnēsia*, a female referent has been ruled out by most modern commentators on linguistic grounds. That may be grammatically responsible, but no one seems to take into account that this grammatical difference did not stop Clement or Origen, native Greek speakers, from suggesting that the referent was a woman. This possibility therefore cannot be excluded, especially given the ways in which social expectation in the ancient Mediterranean world strongly favored the formation of closer emotional bonds with members of the same sex except in the case of close kinship ties. Paul is likely to have thought it fitting to name a woman as third party mediator between two women. Even so, Paul's wife is probably too much of a long shot. Short of the astounding discovery of another document from Paul's time explaining the mystery, we will never know exactly who is intended.

This mysterious third party is asked to help Euodia and

Syntyche, coworkers with Paul and Clement and Paul's other coworkers. Of Clement, nothing more is known. This common Roman name, sometimes connected with a noble Roman family, must have been common enough in a colony with heavy Roman influence. He is someone known to the Philippians but not to us, perhaps another traveling companion of Paul whose name appears nowhere else in his letters, a Philippian by origin. He is surely not the same Clement who appears a generation later as a leading figure in the Roman church.

Most commentators agree that the particular nature of the relative pronoun that introduces the clause about their apostolic labors is not a simple relative but a categorization. The two women are pointed out as belonging in the special category of Paul's coworkers, along with Clement. This too suggests that theirs is not a petty quarrel with no impact on the community, but the central focus of disunity. That their names along with others are written in the "book of life" reflects an old tradition, especially amenable to apocalyptic theology, that a list of the names of those to be saved is kept in heaven (Ps 69:28 [LXX 68:29]; Dan 12:1; Luke 10:20; Rev 3:5; 13:8, etc.).

In contrast to the quite long and complex sentences that Paul writes elsewhere (e.g., 3:8-11, all one sentence in Greek), verses 4-7 are a series of short imperative or hortatory subjunctive constructions, climaxed by a future of result in verse 9. Beginning with verse 4, Paul takes up a different tone, one that is more hopeful that he and they can put behind them the nastiness involved in the quarrel. What follows is the antithesis to the quarreling and divisiveness that characterizes them. Here he returns to the theme of the joy that should characterize Christian life, even in the midst of suffering (see 3:1 and discussion in the introduction about the role of joy in this letter). He tells them that their *epieikes*, that is, their fairness, moderation, forbearance, or gentleness (the last is the NRSV translation), should be made known to everyone, not only in the community, but to every person, including all their nonbelieving social and business contacts. The only way that it will be made known is by the example of their public behavior. This term may have connotations of endurance in a peaceful attitude even in the midst of trial, as a closely related word is used in Wis 2:19; compare its more domesticated use in Titus 3:2, but also a context that approximates this one.

The universality of their responsibility to demonstrate this virtue of moderation may be a reply to the suffering they have had to endure because of their faith (1:29-30). If others see them as sources of joy and mildness, little reason will be found to exert pressure on them because of resentment. The last part of verse 5 contains a somewhat surprising statement: the Lord is near. It is certainly not surprising to hear such statements from Paul, but while there have been eschatological statements in Philippians (1:10; 3:20-21), the apocalyptic perspective has not been dominant. The expression may not apply so much temporally as spiritually, in the sense of some of the Psalms (e.g., 34:18; 119:151; 145:18) in which there is assurance that God will come to the help of those in need (Witherington 1994, 112-13). One gets the impression that Paul is not emphasizing the impending final return of Christ, but that the expression has become habitual for him and is almost unconsciously worked into these verses of encouragement and instruction.

While their gentleness is to be known to everyone (v. 5), this idea is complemented by the statement at the end of verse 6 that their requests are to be made known to God: their gentleness to others, their requests to God. Between these two terms are the assurance not to worry, which follows from the nearness of the Lord in the previous verse, and their prayer and supplication with thanksgiving, *eucharistia,* which has not yet in the Pauline churches become a specific term for what Paul calls the Lord's Supper (1 Cor 11:20; *eucharistia* is used to mean a prayer of thanksgiving in 1 Cor 14:16). The reference to "hearts and minds" at the end of verse 7 is not to be thought of by the modern Western reader as a division between feeling and thinking. Biblical writers did not make such a distinction. Rather, the heart *(kardia)* is the center of the personality that includes both feeling and thinking. It is the core from which all personal initiatives rise. The addition of another word for thoughts *(noēmata)* refers more to the way in which deliberations, once conceived, are worked through and carried out. The peace of God that accomplishes this protection will be complemented by the God of peace in verse 9.

Verse 8 begins with an expression of summary, not only of the immediately preceding verses, but of the entire ideal of life according to the gospel. Though the construction is slightly different, it is reminiscent of 2:1. In both cases a list of virtues has been embedded into a statement that is more expansive and formal than a list but has the same general effect. Verse 9 returns to the imitation theme without using the explicit language (see 3:17). Rather, it spells out how they can imitate him by means of what they have absorbed in four aspects, not necessarily distinct but separated for literary effect: what he has taught them, what they have picked up without formal teaching, and what has come to them through the double senses of hearing and sight.

◊ ◊ ◊ ◊

Verses 4-9 evoke the finest ideals of life according to the gospel. No anxiety or worry, but only confident prayer, all the while living with others in such a way that they are impressed by the sense of peace and gentleness shown by believers. Meanwhile, the sense of quiet joy pervades everything. Here Paul seeks to paint a picture of what life could be like for the Philippians if only they would listen to him and take him as an example. The portrait he paints is of course an ideal, to which readers look in hopes of finding something of it in their own lives, filled with turmoil and stress. Undoubtedly, the Philippians received it in the same way.

A Note of Thanks and a Conclusion (4:10-23)

For advocates of a multiple-letter composition of Philippians, verses 10-20 constitute a distinct letter, written as soon as Paul had received the gift of money from Philippi, carried by Epaphroditus (v. 18; see discussion of fragment theories in the introduction). According to this argument, the fact that the actual saying of thanks and acknowledgment of the gift comes so late in the letter is proof that this is a separate letter, because otherwise Paul would have put the thanks up front. Others find this not at all a problem; he waits until this significant moment at the end of the letter, after he has dealt with the problem of dissension that climaxes at 4:2-3.

◊ ◊ ◊ ◊

Paul's first statement (v. 10) is a typical Pauline sentence in which he throws together several different thoughts without clear distinctions. It leaves us with a mixed impression. He is happy that they have finally revived their concern for him. The verb *anathallein* really means "to bloom again," like flowers in spring that had been as good as dead in winter. Then he sounds as if he is trying to convince himself that the readers really were concerned about him all along, even if they did not show it. Proponents of the friendship theme argue that these lines are simply typical of the letter of friendship: rejoicing at receiving expressions of concern, and assurance to the other that any perceived neglect has not been injurious to the relationship. But the enigmatic statement of verse 10 has led some commentators to think that the source of the dissension in Philippi either created so much chaos that Paul went unnoticed for a time, or that it was the result of divisions about whether or not they should support him. Just in this one fleeting allusion, we are led to think that, contrary to Paul's effusion about the Philippians in the rest of the letter, all has not always been well between him and them. The connector between the two statements of concern, translated "indeed" in the NRSV, is the difficult *eph' hō* (see comment on 3:12), so that there is really a tighter relationship between the two statements than is suggested in the translation. It is more like "inasmuch as you (really) were concerned about me." The language for "concern" is the familiar *phronein* (1:7; 2:2, 5; 3:15 and elsewhere), which we have previously understood as having a certain attitude or orientation. The same meaning applies here.

Paul quickly asserts at the end of verse 10 that they had no chance, no previous opportunity, to show their care for him. Does he say this to excuse them for what he feels was neglect? He then goes on to reassure them that he can be indifferent to need. This leaves us with the impression that they knew for some time of his need before they acted on it. The gift that they did finally send was undoubtedly monetary. Ordinarily such a gift would be used for further missionary travel (Rom 15:24). In this situation of imprisonment, however, the funds would be welcome for a different purpose: to bribe the guards to allow greater freedom, especially about receiving visitors. Early Christian sources like the letters of Ignatius and the *Acts of Perpetua and Felicitas* reveal that this was the ordinary way of dealing with jailors. When Paul speaks in the beginning of the letter of how the word has spread in spite of his chains, to the whole *praetorium* and beyond (1:12-14), he alludes to the possibility of preaching and other kinds of evangelistic contacts. He may there be giving the Philippians a report on how their money has been spent!

In verses 11-12, Paul expresses the ideal of *autarkeia,* even calling himself *autarkēs* (translated "content"). The word really means something closer to "self-sufficiency" (literally, "self-rule"), but New Testament translators are reluctant to render the word this way because, of course, Paul did not use it in an individualist or even autonomous sense. The ideal of self-sufficiency and resultant indifference to pain or pleasure, abundance or want, is a Stoic idealization of the philosopher who has reduced needs and wants to such a minimum as to be truly free of outside constraints (cf. use of the same word in 1 Tim 6:6; a similar idea in 2 Cor 9:8). While discussions of friendship in the genre of letters of friendship sometimes included such ideals, and so the immediate influence could be the friendship tradition, still the ultimate inspiration must be Stoicism, one of the most popular and prevalent philosophical systems of the day. For instance, the freedman Stoic philosopher Epictetus two generations after Paul wrote that his hero Diogenes could love everyone but yet be perfectly content wherever he was, even taken captive by pirates and sold into slavery, because he knew that nothing was his anyway, and that freedom can still be had even in external slavery (*Discourses* 3.24.64-75).

Paul uses the terminology, then turns it around, because it is not himself he relies on, but God or Christ (v. 13), just as later he prays that not they themselves but God will fill in what they need (v. 19). It is not clear here in verse 13 whether God or Christ is the one who strengthens Paul. While the agency of God in verse 19 might suggest that God is intended here, the reference to the power of Christ's resurrection in 3:10 suggests that Christ is the intended referent. So sure were some early scribes that Christ was meant that several principal ancient manuscripts added his name at the end of the sentence, perhaps under the influence of 1 Tim 1:12.

The point has been made: though Paul welcomes the gift of the Philippians and has deep esteem and affection for them, he is dependent neither on their gift nor on their attention to him, because his sole dependence is on God. When he has good things he uses them; when he doesn't, he doesn't. Lest this affirmation sound too aloof, he adds that he is glad and grateful that they could participate or share in his situation of distress. As they were sharers *(syngkoinōnoi)* in the grace of his imprisonment (1:7), now he uses the related verb for their participation in his distressing situation, his *thlipsis,* a term often related to eschatological suffering and distress. It was already used in 1:17 of the trouble some heterodox teachers have tried to cause him. Here it is the suffering of imprisonment but for the sake of the gospel, and thus with ultimate eschatological orientation even if it does not refer primarily to apocalyptic upheaval.

Verses 10-14, therefore, contain much useful information about the nature of the recent communication between Paul and the Philippians—if only we knew how to decode it correctly. The allusions and innuendoes leave much room for speculation, but no clarity. Probably in large part, these are the literary flourishes of one who writes in the friendship tradition and there is no shadow side to the exchange. On the other hand, there may be just a hint of the expression of understandable feelings of abandonment on the part of one imprisoned with uncertain outcome, feeling that the whole world has forgotten him.

Verses 15-18 speak more specifically about the gift received and about the previous generosity of the Philippians, who are addressed with affection in verse 15. In keeping with the Latin influence in Philippi, they are addressed by the Latinized form of the title, *Philippēsioi* based on the Latin *Philippenses,* whereas a more Greek form of their name would be *Philippēnoi* or *Philippeis.* These verses contain several examples of financial vocabulary, undoubtedly used more figuratively than directly, for after all the displays of affection contained earlier in the letter, Paul is surely not speaking as an accountant or banker here. The first of these terms in verse 15 has already been pervasive throughout the letter: *koinōnia.* But it has been argued, particularly by Paul Sampley (1980), that the use of the word here is the central one and that it represents a Greek translation of the Latin *societas,* a particular kind of Roman business partnership agreement among equals for a specific end. It is doubtful, however, whether the adaptation of a business agreement dominated the relationship of Paul and the Philippians, and it has never been adequately demonstrated that *koinōnia* is the Greek equivalent of *societas* in business language, though in certain contexts it did carry connotations of financial exchange (see further discussion in the introduction).

The second piece of would-be business language, repeated at the end of verse 17, is "in the matter of" *(eis logon),* which can technically mean "into the account of" (NRSV: "to your account"). The third is "giving and receiving" *(dosis kai lēmpsis),* meaning regular exchange or debits and credits (see Sir 41:19 [41:21 LXX]; 42:7). Another is the "profit" or "return" or therefore "interest" (literally "fruit," *karpos*) that accrues to their account because of their gift in verse 17. Yet another is *apechō,* "I have been paid in full," the language of a business receipt in verse 18. Taken all together, they present a formidable set of formal financial language, all of which is well attested in business documents. Does this then mean that after three chapters of friendship language, Paul now gets down to business, or that if this is another letter added here, it is of an entirely different genre? The language in this section is not only businesslike, but there is affection as well: Paul reminds them that only they offered to connect with him in the early days when he first left them and went down the road to Thessalonica, a statement designed to flatter appropriately, and so perhaps not to be taken completely literally. Verse 17 is playful and affectionate, and verse 18 escapes from business language into liturgical metaphors. Recent scholars have collected good evidence that other writers such as Cicero, Seneca, Epictetus, and Plutarch used such business language in contexts of friendship and social exchange (some references in O'Brien 1991, 534; Peterman 1997, 205-7). In one of the examples, Cicero (*De amicitia* 16.58) criticizes the idea that friendship can exist on the exact reciprocity of credits and debits *(ratio acceptorum et datorum);* rather, it must be more flexible. This is a good indication that Paul too used these financial terms metaphorically as a medium for social exchange.

Paul gratefully recalls their generosity, more than once, on his previous visit to Macedonia (v. 16), careful to add, in keeping with his stated indifference and personal freedom from material things in verses 11-12, that his object was not so much the gift as the benefit accruing to them, the interest it would bear for them, for their good deed—a clever rhetorical twist (v. 17). This express admission that Paul accepted gifts from the Philippians several times for his support and the furtherance of his mission stands in tension with his adamant insistence in 1 Corinthians that he accepted nothing from them, but earned his own keep, in spite of his right to be supported by a community he was serving (1 Cor 9:3-18)—though later in the same letter he does seem to hint that he would accept money for his further travel (1 Cor 16:6). It prompts the question: Which custom, accepting support or rejecting it, was Paul's usual practice? Which is the ordinary and which the exception? In 4:15 Paul says that no one else in Macedonia offered him gifts. He does not say that was true everywhere he went. But because of his peculiar and tumultuous relationship with the Corinthians, perhaps only there he renounced all gifts or support in order to preserve his independence. The reader cannot help remarking what a different tone characterizes his dealings with the Corinthians and the Philippians.

Verse 18 switches the metaphorical location from the bank to the temple, where their gift is now not a business deal but a sacrifice pleasing to God. While modern readers have great difficulty imagining that the smell of burning flesh could be pleasing to anyone except on a slow barbecue, the "fragrant offering" or "pleasing smell" of sacrifice is as old in biblical literature as Gen 8:21; Exod 29:18; and Ezek 20:41. Very similar language appears in Eph 5:2, where it is the self-sacrifice of Christ that is a fragrant offering and sacrifice to God. Paul has previously used similar sacrificial language in this letter to speak of the possibility of his own demise as a libation on their sacrifice (2:17). The "fragrant offering" is *osmē euōdias,* the second word differing only by the long omega from *Euodia,* the name of one of the key players in verse 2. A play on words may be intended, but the expression was familiar enough that Paul may not have noticed the pun.

One further reference to financial matters occurs in the prayerful wish of verse 19, where Paul promises that God will supply everything they need from divine wealth, obviously a metaphorical allusion. There is an implicit call to conversion here. In chapter 3, Paul sought to embed in his hearers the habit of imitating him. In 4:11-12 he presents himself as one who can "take it or leave it" when it comes to possessions and resources. Now he promises that God's riches are enough for anybody. The Philippians, too, are called to the indifference and Christ-sufficiency that Paul has proposed. The formal brief prayer of praise or doxology of verse 20 is unexpectedly unitarian (cf. 1:2; 1 Cor 1:3; 2 Cor 1:2; Gal 1:3; 1 Thess 1:1), though Christ has just been mentioned along with God in the previous verse. It concludes with the Aramaic acclamation "Amen" that we know from this and other sources (Rom 1:25; 1 Cor 14:16; Gal 1:5; Jude 25; Rev 5:14, etc.) was very early introduced even into Greek prayer as the way to express affirmation and assent to what was said.

The brief conclusion to the letter, verses 21-23, follows the expected form of the hellenistic letter by sending greetings from those whom the recipients might know. It repeats Paul's opening and frequently used greeting to the saints or holy ones (see discussion of the meaning at 1:1). No distinction is to be understood between the saints of verse 21a, 22 and the "friends" (literally "brothers") of verse 21*b*. The "emperor's household" (literally the "household of Caesar") refers to the network of imperial civil servants, mostly slaves and freedmen, throughout the empire and does not require a Roman location for the writing of the letter (see further discussion in the introduction). The final prayer-blessing is uniquely christological, as is Paul's customary way of concluding a letter (Rom 16:20; 1 Cor 16:23; Gal 6:18; 1 Thess 5:28). Here and in Gal 6:18, he changes the simple "you" plural to "your spirit" *(pneuma),* in which "your" is plural but "spirit" is singular. This may be a simple collective singular and be directed at the personal spirit of each recipient, or it may refer to the common spirit that animates the community, still, however, a reference to the human, not the divine, spirit.

Several qualities come through at nearly every point of this letter: friendship, joy, desire for unity, and hope. Despite the recognized stereotypes of epistolary expression present here, not only Paul's esteem but his genuine affection for the Philippians comes through. This is especially clear when the letter is compared to most other Pauline letters in which the emotional distance between Paul and his recipients is noticeably greater. His true joy in the midst of a very difficult and uncertain situation is one of the most remarkable things about this letter. This joy that Paul has found in his confinement for Christ is contagious: He wants to share it with them and leave it with them as a permanent legacy. But more than anything else, he wants them to be united in their common faith, table, and hope for the future. Without unity, there can be no preparedness for the day of the Lord. Without the communion of unity, they cannot strengthen their internal bonds in the way necessary to wait in hope for the transformation that will bring them to their true home.

INTRODUCTION: PHILEMON

It is worth pondering how this remarkable gem ever made it into the New Testament canon. With the exception of 2 Timothy, generally judged by modern scholars to be pseudepigraphical, this is the only seemingly "private" or "personal" letter of Paul that has survived. Yet it is receiving more attention today than at any other time in the history of biblical interpretation, with the possible exception of the antebellum abolitionist era in the United States. Perhaps the letter was considered to have timeless value because it was from Paul himself, perhaps because of its subject matter, or perhaps because the ascription is not only to Philemon but to the whole church that meets in the house he shares with Apphia and Archippus (v. 1).

STRUCTURE

The *address* or *prescript* (vv. 1-3) is followed by a brief *thanksgiving* (vv. 4-7). The *body* of the letter (vv. 8-16) and the recapitulation of the argument (vv. 17-20) end with a *conclusion* (vv. 21-25).

LITERARY AFFINITIES

There are a number of factors that the letter shares with Philippians. Here too Paul is a prisoner (vv. 1, 9-10, 13). Timothy is also present (v. 1; Phil 2:19-24). He had also been with Paul in Phil 2:19, so the circumstances of imprisonment may be the same.

Paul hopes to visit the letter's recipients again (v. 22) as in Phil 1:26. This fits with a possible Ephesian imprisonment earlier in Paul's apostolic career than at the time of his final arrest (see the introduction to Philippians). There is also some kind of connection with Colossians. Every name that appears in the letter to Philemon, with the exceptions of Philemon and Apphia (v. 1), appears also in Colossians: Archippus (v. 1; Col 4:17), Epaphras (v. 23; Col 4:12), Mark and Aristarchus (v. 23; Col 4:10), Onesimus (v. 10; Col 4:9), and Demas and Luke (v. 24; Col 4:14). Jesus called Justus (Col 4:11) may also be mentioned in Phlm 23 (see comment there). This affinity of names suggests a location somewhere in the Lycus Valley near Colossae, perhaps the city of Colossae itself, or nearby Laodicea, both about one hundred miles from the west coast of Asia Minor with easy access to the coastal cities. This location would strengthen the theory of an Ephesian imprisonment as context for the writing of both Philippians and Philemon. The date of the letter would then be in the mid-50s. But John Knox's proposal (1959) that Philemon is really the lost letter of Paul to the Laodiceans (Col 4:15-16) has gained few followers.

SITUATION

Paul in prison writes to Philemon, Apphia, and Archippus and to the *ekklēsia* in their house (v. 1). The letter is therefore semi-public, intended to be read in the assembly of the house-church, even though the business in it concerns only Philemon. This is evidenced by the fact that immediately after the greeting, beginning in verse 4, the second-person singular is introduced and remains throughout the letter until the final verse.

Onesimus is not Philemon's emissary; the plea for Philemon to receive him is careful and prolonged (vv. 15-17). Rather, Onesimus has come to Paul without Philemon's knowledge for whatever reason, and Paul has sent him back with this letter of mediation. There is a strong likelihood that Philemon is not happy with Onesimus for some reason: verse 18 is not just a rhetorical flourish in the remote possibility that something unpleasant has happened between them, but a delicate way to talk about at least Paul's perception that Philemon will not be pleased to see Onesimus. A new relationship has come about between Paul and Onesimus during the visit (v. 10), probably the baptism of Onesimus, though some other kind of changed relationship is also possible, such as Onesimus's determination to become an apostle like Paul (see Phil 2:22 for similar parental language about Timothy). If baptism is intended in verse 10, which is most likely, this is a good example of the autonomy of household slaves to make their own decisions about conversion even where the *paterfamilias* is Christian, a different pattern than we see in the stories of mass household conversions described in Acts (e.g., Acts 10:44-48; 16:33). Paul wants to keep Onesimus for ministry work with him, but sends him back first for reconciliation with Philemon and his approval for this new work. Paul asks Philemon to accept a new level of relationship with Onesimus, probably including the manumission of his slave.

There are four current theories that attempt to fill in the details of the story, and some of them run contrary to the above summary.

1. One of the earliest interpreters of Philemon was John Chrysostom in the still slave-owning society of the late–fourth century. Though Mitchell (1995) has shown that Chrysostom's interpretation was common at the time, it has become the traditional one: Onesimus is a runaway slave who fortuitously finds Paul during his flight. Paul baptizes him and convinces him to return to his master with Paul's mediating letter of recommendation. Philemon is thus placed in the awkward position of having everyone in the assembly know what Paul is asking of him, to take back his runaway slave as a brother, even though by custom and law Onesimus should be severely punished. Philemon is under strong pressure from Paul, with the knowledge of the whole house-church for which he serves as patron, to ignore outside social expectations that would prompt him to be severe with a runaway slave, even one who voluntarily returns. If Philemon does not maintain his honor by exacting punishment, however,

his neighbors and friends will cry that "family values" are falling apart because proper household discipline is not preserved.

This traditional interpretation is not without problems. It is never expressly said either that Onesimus is a slave or that he has run away. And it is difficult to see how Paul and Onesimus "just happened" to encounter each other and how Paul has the freedom and authority to send back a runaway slave to his owner when this would really be a matter for the authorities. It is possible that Onesimus was captured and is being returned forcibly, but with Paul's letter to mitigate the situation.

2. One of the first to question the runaway theory was Peter Lampe (1985), who proposed, based on passages from the Roman legal codes, that Onesimus has knowingly fled from the house of Philemon because of conflict between them, but has fled to a friendly third party, Paul, to intercede for him with Philemon. In the legal discussions of such a case, the slave is not to be considered a *fugitivus* or runaway, subject to legal penalties. This interpretation would certainly fit the implied circumstances if Onesimus is absent without official leave, and makes more sense of what is otherwise a remarkable coincidence: that Onesimus just happened to encounter Paul in another city. Paul's carefully composed letter then serves the exact function for which Onesimus came to Paul: to intercede for him with his owner Philemon.

A literary parallel that is often cited, and which fits especially well with this interpretation, is Pliny's letter 9.21 to Sabinianus (text in Lohse 1971, 196-97 n. 2), urging a reconciliation between him and his freedman, who has somehow grievously offended and has come to Pliny to intercede with his patron and former owner. Pliny's letter 9.24 is a follow-up after the reconciliation has taken place, thanking and congratulating Sabinianus for his acquiescence. Would that we had such a follow-up letter from Paul to let us know the outcome of that situation. Both of Pliny's letters use persuasion remarkably similar to that of Paul in the letter to Philemon, even to the point of specifically reminding the recipient of the requester's authority, which will not be needed because the recipient will comply voluntarily (Letter 9.24; cf. Phlm 8-9, 19).

Lampe's interpretation has been defended and augmented by Scott Bartchy (1992) and Brian Rapske (1991) but seriously questioned by J. Albert Harrill (1999) who cautions against assuming that the opinions of legal theorists had much to do with actual social practice.

3. More recently, Sara Winter has argued four points, partially influenced by Knox (1959). First, because of the large number of legal and commercial terms typical of public documents, the letter is intended for the whole church, not just Philemon or the three named in the prescript. Second, Onesimus, slave not of Philemon but of Archippus, did not run away but rather was sent to Paul on behalf of the church at Colossae. Third, Paul writes to get Onesimus released from work in Colossae in order to stay in ministry with Paul. Onesimus is not the bearer of the letter back to Colossae. Finally, Paul clearly expects that Onesimus will be manumitted for this new work.

Points one, three, and four have much to commend them, though the arguments are not watertight. The second point, that Onesimus is in fact an emissary of the church to Paul, is difficult to reconcile with verses 11, 15, and 18. It is not clear why Paul would make a negative pun on the "useful" meaning of Onesimus's name if he were an official representative of the church. Nor would Paul refer to a separation between the two if it was planned that way. Most of all, verse 18 with its suggestion of Onesimus's wrongdoing in need of forgiveness does not sit well with his responsibility as agent of the church.

4. More recently still, Allen Callahan (1997) has revived an interpretation previously proposed by abolitionists in the antebellum United States. The traditional interpretation of this letter along with the exhortations to slaves' obedience in the household codes and later in the New Testament (Eph 6:5-8; Col 3:22-25; 1 Tim 6:1-2; Titus 2:9-10; 1 Pet 2:18-25) was used to support the argument that the Bible approved of slavery. The new interpretation that was offered rejects the identification of Onesimus as a slave. The only definite indication from which to conclude of Onesimus's servile status is verse 16, which Callahan argues has been exploited since the late–fourth century by powerful interests

in slave-owning societies against its real meaning in order to justify theirs. This alternate interpretation must also rely almost entirely on verse 16, but with the opposite conclusion: Onesimus is really Philemon's brother (the real meaning of "in the flesh") who has been grossly mistreated by Philemon and has fled for help from the family house to Paul. Paul urges Philemon to take back Onesimus and stop treating him as if he were a slave, but to start treating him like what he really is: a beloved brother. Thus the letter is not about slavery at all, but about relationships among blood kin.

Callahan is right to raise the question all over again, for biblical interpretation must always reexamine old assumptions. The problem here is that exegesis may be driven by one understanding of biblical authority. If what biblical persons say and do becomes normative and limiting of what contemporary readers can think and do, then exegesis cannot function freely. But if we can allow biblical persons to be part of their own world with a quite different worldview than ours, then the situation is different. Slavery was as much a part of the ancient Mediterranean world as the Holocaust, nuclear warfare, abortion, and capital punishment are of ours. It is highly likely that a future generation will look at our age and consider us just as barbarous for allowing such practices as we do early Christians for their acceptance of slavery. If Onesimus was a slave, then Paul does take slavery for granted as part of his world (which is not at all the same thing as approving of it), as did most of his Christian contemporaries and successors for several centuries. He does so, however, with a certain ambiguity (1 Cor 7:21) and probably with a bias toward manumission (Phlm 16). If today we rightly abhor slavery as unconscionable, we must also be prepared to accept the fact that it took a long time for Christians to come to that conclusion. It is tragic that biblical texts have been used to justify social injustice of any kind, but such misuse does not invalidate exegetical conclusions or the need to look directly at original social contexts. On the other hand, extreme caution must be exercised against simply accepting a traditional interpretation and rejecting a newer one because it shatters long-held assumptions.

Until a few years ago, scholars would have stated with confidence that the social situation behind the writing of Philemon was the case of a runaway slave, but recent newer theories have cast serious doubt on this traditional assumption. The dust will have to settle for a few years before we will be able to see whether the newer interpretations will command lasting credibility.

In the early decades of the second century, Ignatius of Antioch wrote to several churches of western Asia Minor on his way to martyrdom in Rome. At that time, Ephesus had a bishop named Onesimus (Ign. *Eph.* 1.3). It is tempting to see in this Onesimus the later career of our member of Philemon's household, but the stretch of time is probably too great.

Assuming that Onesimus was a slave recently baptized by Paul under whatever circumstances, this situation raises for Paul, Philemon, and the rest of the Christian tradition the serious question, How do baptism and membership in the church change relationships? That question will be pursued at further length in the commentary.

COMMENTARY: PHILEMON

ADDRESS (1-3)

Paul opens by identifying himself not as apostle but prisoner of Jesus Christ, immediately establishing not only his actual situation (see also vv. 9-10, 13) but also its meaning for him in relationship to his following of Christ. This is the only letter in which Paul describes himself thus in the opening line (but see vv. 9-10, 13; Eph 3:1; 2 Tim 1:8). His choice of this title for himself may also support the interpretation that Onesimus is a slave, and Paul seeks for rhetorical effect to identify himself in some way with the status of Onesimus, though calling himself the "slave of Christ" as in Rom 1:1 or Phil 1:1 would have been more effective for that purpose. Or perhaps Paul avoids the term *doulos* (slave) for himself to distinguish his status from that of Onesimus. The address is *from* two persons, Paul and Timothy, yet from verse 4 Paul alone speaks. The address is *to* three persons, yet from verse 2 Paul speaks only to one, usually understood to be the first named in the address, Philemon. The first use of the second-person singular occurs in verse 2, "the church in *your* house" (emphasis added), immediately after the introduction of the third name, Archippus. John Knox (1959) argued because of this immediate mention of the house-church after Archippus and because of Paul's description of Archippus as "our fellow soldier," that the leader of the house-church and addressee of the letter was really Archippus and not Philemon (62-70). The argument is plausible but it is more likely that the first person named is the addressee intended in the rest of the letter. Each of the three characters has some ascription. Philemon is "our dear friend" (literally, "beloved") and "coworker," probably of Paul and Timothy (see Rom 16:3, 9 and discussion of this term at Phil 4:3). Apphia is called "sister," and Archippus "fellow soldier," a term that Paul also uses for Epaphroditus (Phil 2:25), probably for those who have had some history of struggle or suffering for the faith. In Col 4:17, Archippus is given a solemn warning to fulfill a specific ministry entrusted to him by the Lord, but no further details are known.

We would like to know the relationship of these three people to one another and to Paul, but we will never know for certain. It is possible that Apphia is Philemon's wife and Archippus his brother, or that all three are unmarried siblings in the same household, or if married, their spouses do not share the faith. It is less likely that Apphia is the wife of Archippus, since wives would not normally be named before their husbands (but see Prisca and Aquila in Acts 18:26; Rom 16:3; 2 Tim 4:19 in contrast to 1 Cor 16:19). Of course, it is also possible that only one of the three hosts the house-church and the other two are the only other members of it that Paul knows. If Onesimus is Philemon's brother as Allen Callahan (1997) argues, the addressees would be aware that his name is conspicuously missing from the list. Perhaps the two men, Philemon and Archippus, have a history of apostolic work known to Paul that Apphia does not share, for Paul is not reluctant to name women who have worked in ministerial roles (e.g., Rom 16:3, 6, 12; Phil 4:2-3), and his title for her is the simple way that he would address any female believer. What we can say for certain is that the house is in the name of one person, most likely Philemon, since the house is referred to in verse 2 as "your (singular) house." Verse 3 is a typical conclusion to a Pauline address. It is verbatim as that in Rom 1:7; 1 Cor 1:3; Eph 1:2; Col 1:2 in some manuscripts; and Phil 1:2, thus a familiar Pauline usage.

THANKSGIVING (4-7)

The thanksgiving formula is typical of any Pauline letter, telling the recipient that he is always remembered in Paul's intercessory prayer, and praising his outstanding virtues, in this case love and faith. It speaks of the sharing of faith (v. 6), where the word for sharing is *koinōnia,* an important term for the relationships between Paul and the community and of members of the community with one another; so too, here. The section concludes with the statement that the hearts or affective capacities (*ta splangchna;* see Phil 1:8) of the holy ones, that is, believers, have been refreshed because of what Philemon has done. The expression is a difficult one to translate, but connotes enthusiasm and affective energy. The reference is probably to his hosting of the house-church, which included providing the necessary patronage for what could have been a very mixed group, as well as hospitality to visiting believers (v. 22) and a center for religious instruction and missionary training. Thus Paul may be alluding not only to the members of that immediate group, but also to many others who have passed through and benefited from the hospitality offered there.

BODY OF THE LETTER (8-16)

After the appropriate opening praise, the purpose for writing begins to unfold at verse 8. The letter is a masterpiece of persuasive rhetoric, and Paul's skill at this art is quickly apparent. Many modern readers find the letter distastefully manipulative because of our different standards of direct communication. But this was the ancient ideal: an argument so well crafted that the addressee could not refuse. Paul presents himself as one qualified to command by authority, yet he would prefer asking through love (v. 9). He appeals under two of his own roles, that of elder and prisoner. His self-ascription as elder need not necessarily mean that he is chronologically older than Philemon, though he may be. It is, rather, a title of honor, meaning senior member, probably carrying with it a connotation of authority. The word used here, *presbytēs,* has stronger connotations of elder in rank or age than the closely related *presbyteros,* sometimes used in the New Testament for a member of a council of elders in charge of a church or group of churches (Acts 11:30; 14:23; 20:17; Titus 1:5; Jas 5:14; 1 Pet 5:1). He appeals too as more recently a prisoner (as in v. 1). He does not seek to explain the circumstances of his imprisonment, an indication that it is not news to Philemon and his church, and therefore that there is probably not too great a geographical distance between Paul and the church.

The heart of the appeal is introduced at verse 10 and following, using the kinship language that Paul often finds appropriate (see especially Phil 2:22). In this case it is paternal imagery that is used, for Paul talks of himself as having begotten Onesimus in prison, probably meaning that he has brought Onesimus to the faith and ultimately to baptism, though it is also possible that some other kind of conversion is meant, in which Onesimus acquires a new spiritual élan and identity, perhaps discovery of an apostolic vocation or a willingness to return home and confront the consequences of his less-than-ideal behavior. Paul appeals as a social equal on his behalf to one who holds authority over Onesimus. Given the context, the appeal must be intercessory, not a request to keep Onesimus with Paul, as Winter (1987) argues on linguistic bases.

In verse 11 Paul works a play on the name, Onesimus, which means "useful," by employing another word with the same meaning in both its negative and positive forms. There may be a further pun intended, too: in hellenistic Greek (and modern Greek as well), the word *chrēstos* ("useful") would have been pronounced exactly like *christos* ("anointed one," or Christ). Thus "useless" *(achrēstos)* could also be heard as "without Christ," Onesimus's situation before baptism (Lohse 1971, 200). Confusion of the two words was easy. There is a running disagreement among historians about whether the riots that took place in the Roman-Jewish community about 49 CE *impulsore chresto* (at the instigation of an otherwise unknown person named Chrestus) were in fact caused by animosity against Christians and their leader, Christus (Suetonius, *Claudius* 25.4).

Against the argument that there is no alienation between Onesimus and Philemon but rather that one is actually sent by the other, it is difficult to justify the negative pun unless there is a negative judgment in the air about Onesimus. Against the hypothesis that Onesimus is the brother of Philemon, it must be said that in the first century, slaves were often given demeaning names signifying their value to their owners. Onesimus is thus a typical slave's name, like Tychikos and Fortunatus ("lucky") or Felix ("happy"), which appear so commonly. In later centuries, the distinctiveness of slave and free names became blurred. It is also unlikely, if Onesimus were the social equal of Philemon, that Paul would make such a condescending pun on his name.

The verb of sending in verse 12 is *anapempein* in the epistolary aorist with present meaning. Its ordinary meaning is to "send back," as it is usually taken here. On occasion in legal contexts, the verb can mean to "send up" or "refer" to a higher authority (as in Luke 23:7 and perhaps vv. 11, 15, though these are ambiguous; Acts 25:21). Some following Knox (1959) would argue that that is its meaning here. If so, then Paul is using legal language to say that he refers the matter of Onesimus's disposition to the one to whom that decision belongs, Philemon. If this is so, then there is no evidence that Onesimus is being sent back to Philemon or thus that he carries the letter. Most commentators, however, understand the meaning here to be that Paul is sending Onesimus back to Philemon. The conclusion of verse 12 is difficult to translate. Again the word *splangchna* is used. Perhaps something like "He is my own heart" or "a substitute for me" would be appropriate. This personal addition makes little sense if the first part of the sentence does not mean that Paul is sending Onesimus back to Philemon, for how would Paul "send up" or "refer" his own heart? He is hardly placing himself with Onesimus under the judgment of Philemon. In this verse we can see part of the situation: Onesimus has, perhaps unexpectedly, turned up at the doorstep of Philemon's house carrying Paul's letter. Lest Philemon be inclined to be severe, Paul is letting him know how precious Onesimus is to him.

Paul states in verse 13 that he would like to have Onesimus remain with him while Paul is in prison, and one of his functions there would be to remind Paul of Philemon and to represent him. This is a rhetorical strategy. It does not mean that Onesimus has been sent by Philemon as his representative. Philemon, Paul hints, would of course be there himself if he could; this is one of the clever rhetorical turns that signals to the loyal follower or friend what he should be thinking. Onesimus's ideal role, if he were to stay with Paul, is expressed in a form of the verb *diakonein*, which is often assumed to mean something like the service of a personal attendant. However, its most usual meaning is the service of some kind of official representation or agency of an important person, in this case Paul or Christ. As the terminology evolved in early Christianity to mean "ministry," it carried those connotations.

Thus the statement in verse 14 that Onesimus could be there with Paul on behalf of Philemon widens the representative role. In Christian literature the language of *diakonia* most often has to do with some kind of ministry, perhaps that of preaching or consoling. It seems then that at Onesimus's conversion and baptism, a promising possible path had opened up before him, that of laboring in the ministry side by side with Paul. Additionally, he would serve as a reminder of Philemon's supposed desire to do the same. But for some other reason, Paul has decided at least temporarily to send Onesimus back to Philemon, perhaps to receive the blessing of his patron Philemon on this new endeavor, but perhaps too to bring about a reconciliation if one was needed. This verse is once again an indication of Paul's mastery of persuasive rhetoric: By virtue of his own position and authority Paul could have commanded obedience (v. 21), yet he wants, rather, to give Philemon the chance to do a good deed freely and willingly.

Paul suggests in verse 15 that there is a divine plan to all of this, and Onesimus and Philemon were separated for awhile—not smoothly, one suspects—so that they might resume their relationship in a new way. There is a double contrast in the statement: separation for a time versus having forever. Of course, if Paul expects Philemon to send Onesimus back to work with him (v. 13), then they will be separated again. The reunion of which Paul speaks is on a deeper level, which reinforces the suspicion that the separation was not the result of a pleasant departure. There is a true conversion of attitude to be undergone, the content of which is expressed by Paul in verse 16 in a way that leaves the outside reader guessing about his real intention.

Verse 16 is a hinge text for many interpretations of the situation as well as for the theological question of Paul's dealing with slavery. This is the sole verse that presumably identifies Onesimus literally as a slave and figuratively as a potential brother. Yet Callahan has argued just the opposite, that Onesimus is truly Philemon's blood brother while the reference to slavery is figurative. Philemon has been treating his brother slavishly and is asked to stop it. In this interpretation, Onesimus is indeed a brother "in the flesh" in the most literal way. Now he is to be treated as a brother "in the Lord" as well. What suggests a different meaning in the passage itself is Paul's side comment that he has the same relationship to Onesimus, who is also his beloved brother. This is difficult to reconcile with an actual blood relationship between Onesimus and Philemon, for surely there is not the same between Onesimus and Paul. It is better, therefore, to assume that the brotherly allusion means something else.

It was common for Pauline Christians to call each other brother and sister. Would slaves and owners use those titles for each other and see each other in that way? That would have been a stretch, one to which perhaps Philemon is being called. If Onesimus has only recently been baptized while with Paul, his relationship with Philemon has necessarily changed, at least in Paul's view. Philemon is called to see Onesimus in a new way, no longer only "in the flesh," that is, for what they both are humanly and historically, but also "in the Lord," for whom "there is no longer slave or free" (Gal 3:28). For Winter, "the recipient of the letter will 'own' Onesimus fully when he receives him in Christ as a brother" (1987, 10). Whether this necessarily presumes manumission is not clear because in the whole passage it is never clear whether the social or spiritual dimension is at issue, or both. Other later statements that may suggest manumission are verses 17 and 21. While to the modern reader it seems inconceivable that Onesimus could continue as a slave, we know that slavery was tolerated by Christians for centuries more.

RECAPITULATION (17-20)

Verse 17 may have some connection to the above discussion, but perhaps not. It may be more revelatory of the relationship between Paul and Philemon, his "dear friend and coworker" (v. 1), with whom he says he is *koinōnon*, that is, equal associate or partner. (See discussion of the *koinōnia* word group in Philippians.) Paul asks Philemon to receive Onesimus as he would Paul. It has been argued that this is the statement that indicates Paul's expectation that Philemon will manumit Onesimus, but it need not be. If the model of a consensual *societas* or partnership lies behind the terminology, slaves too could belong to such partnerships. Paul's request that Philemon receive Onesimus as he would receive Paul, however, might simply mean that Paul wants Philemon to consider him as if he were Paul's fully authorized representative agent, or *diakonos* in one of the original meanings of the word.

It is difficult to read verse 18 without forming the conclusion that there is something wrong between Philemon and Onesimus— or at least that Paul thinks there is, and where else would he have formed that judgment other than from Onesimus? The legal language by which Paul tells Philemon to charge anything to his account is more than raising a possibility contrary to fact. It is obviously not meant literally, nor need it mean that there has been destruction or theft of material property, though that is not excluded. Paul suggests the possibility (a polite way of bringing up the topic) that Onesimus has "wronged" *(ēdikēsen)* Philemon, that is, has offended against the common sense of justice and honor. Philemon's public honor as a householder has been compromised by some insulting action, and the appeal is to his own deeper personal sense of honor, for he will be more greatly esteemed if he can forgive and reconcile than if he exacts strict justice.

While most of the letter was probably written by a secretary as was true with most of Paul's letters (see Rom 16:22), it was not uncommon at the end for the writer to add the closing lines in his own hand (1 Cor 16:21; Gal 6:11; Col 4:18; 2 Thess 3:17). Paul intervenes here at a crucial point, the point at which he promises to make good on anything yet owed to Philemon. This he puts in his own handwriting, lest there be any doubt that he means it. He probably continues then to write the rest of the letter himself. As he promises full recompense to Philemon, Paul subtly reminds him in the same breath that a debt is owed the other way, presumably because Paul was responsible for Philemon's evangelization and conversion.

In verse 20, Paul speaks of his desire to benefit from Philemon's acquiescence. The verb is *onaimēn,* a rare optative of the verb *oninēmi,* to benefit or take joy in something. It is often taken here to be another pun on the name Onesimus, this time with root connection and assonance as well as meaning, whereas the other pun was carried only by meaning (v. 11). The expression was a favorite of Ignatius of Antioch (Ign. *Eph.* 2.2; Ign. *Magn.* 2.1; 12.1; Ign. *Rom.* 5.2; Ign. *Pol.* 1.1; 6.2). When he visited the Ephesian community more than half a century later, its bishop was a man named Onesimus, probably not the same as the one known by Paul. But the possibility of a pun here is strengthened by Ignatius's apparent use of the expression in his letter to the Ephesians. The fact that it was a favorite expression of Ignatius does not invalidate his ability to use it as a pun. So too with Paul. He concludes the wish with a third use of *splangchna* (see vv. 7, 12), this time relating it explicitly to their common incorporation into Christ.

CONCLUSION (21-25)

Though throughout the letter to this point Paul has made great effort to be polite and diplomatic, hoping to evoke Philemon's generosity, in verse 21 we see the real relationship. As in most Pauline communities, Paul sees himself as the authority who can command—though it does not always work. Everywhere he tries first to persuade, but does assert his authority when he feels it necessary. We have seen the same pattern in Philippians, where Paul first exhorts and appeals to the example of Christ (2:1-11), then at the conclusion of the section, reminds them that their proper response is obedience (2:12). Here too this is simply the final appeal: if nothing else, you will be obedient. Yet even here, the appeal to generosity prevails, for Paul expresses his persuasive confidence that Philemon will do much more than obey: he will apply his imagination to this situation and take the best way out. What that means is left perhaps deliberately vague. As John Barclay (1991) remarks, since we do not know for certain what Paul is asking in the first place, we have no idea what this "more" is supposed to be! Perhaps this is the real hint toward manumission, or toward sending Onesimus back to Paul for good, even laden with a new contribution to the mission. It is also possible that Paul leaves the suggestion so vague because he himself is not sure what is the best course of action, and leaves it for Philemon to discern (Barclay 1991, 174-75).

Whether the expression in verse 22 of Paul's intention to return to Philemon's house is a hope or a "tacit threat . . . just tentative enough to be imminent without being falsifiable" so that Philemon knows Paul intends to carry through personally on the issue (Callahan 1997, 64), it suggests that Paul is in a situation that is not hopeless and in which distance does not seem to be an obstacle. Nor does he expect a very long time to pass before his visit, for the introductory *hama* (NRSV: "one thing more") really suggests in a general sense another thing to be done simultaneously. What Philemon is to prepare for Paul is a *xenia,* usually understood here as a lodging (as in Acts 28:23), but its meaning is broader: a hospitable reception with all the amenities that good hospitality entails. Paul's way of saying that he is coming for a visit is charming: he hopes to be bestowed as a blessing or given as a gift to Philemon and his community *(charisthēsomai).*

Paul seems to have with him quite a circle of coworkers, as evidenced by all the people named in the final greeting, verses 23-24. In Col 4:10, Aristarchus is also a prisoner with Paul; nothing is said of the status of the others. Here only Epaphras is called a fellow prisoner. As has been the case in the entire letter from verse 4, the one greeted in verse 23 is singular. Thus even in these final greetings, only Philemon is addressed. The plural address was given only in verse 3. Both here and in Col 4:10-11, the verb of greeting is a singular with plural subject. The awkwardness of that literary convention is avoided in the NRSV translation by wording it as if only Epaphras sends greetings, then the others are added as an afterthought. In the Greek, there is no equivalent of the NRSV connector, "and so do." The list of additional names follows immediately after the mention of Christ. A comparison of the names in verses 23-24 and Col 4:10-14 reveals that only one name from Colossians is missing in Philemon: Jesus called Justus, a Jew (see Col 4:11) with the common name Jesus who also carries the Roman name Justus, just as the Jew Saul carries the Roman name Paul.

In 1909, the German scholar Ernst Amling proposed that indeed the name of this apostle Jesus is in Philemon 23, too. Instead of "Epaphras, my fellow prisoner in Christ Jesus," which would be the only use of the expression "in Christ Jesus" in the letter (see "for Christ," verse 6; "in Christ," verses 8, 20), it is possible to read "Epaphras, my fellow prisoner in Christ, Jesus, Mark," and so on, so that Jesus is the first in the subsequent list of Mark, Aristarchus, Demas, and Luke. In the NRSV translation, that would mean rearranging the whole sentence, but not in the Greek. It would, however, mean assuming that a final sigma of the nominative form was lost on the name Jesus, now in all manuscripts in the dative case, *Iēsou* instead of *Iēsous* as part of the phrase "in Christ Jesus." That is not a difficult supposition since, if the theory is correct, copyists would be quite likely to assume that the text reads *en Christō Iēsou*, "in Christ Jesus," because the combination of the two names is familiar in Pauline letters. This reading has been adopted by many commentators, but against it is the question of whether Paul himself would not have seen the potential for misunderstanding and put the name Jesus somewhere else in the list if this person had been present with him.

The Epaphras mentioned here appears elsewhere only in Col 1:7; 4:12, unless he is to be identified with Epaphroditus (Phil 2:25; 4:18). This Mark is commonly thought to be the same as John Mark, son of Mary and companion of Barnabas (Acts 12:12, 25; 15:37, 39). Aristarchus also appears as a companion of Paul in Acts 10:29; 20:4; 27:2. Demas has a more checkered history in the tradition, as one who has deserted Paul in 2 Tim 4:10. The later *Acts of Paul* 12 take up that hint to turn him into an opponent of Paul. Just as Philemon is a "coworker" (v. 1), so too are all those named in verses 23-24. The wording does not tell us whether Philemon is acquainted with them, but at least Paul suggests that they all have in common the mission of the Gospel.

The final blessing is a simple wish that Christ be with them, as is common in the conclusions of Pauline letters. Here the wish for Christ's presence is "with your spirit" as in Gal 6:18; Phil 4:23, rather than the more usual "with you," but the meaning is the same (see comment on Phil 4:23).

◊ ◊ ◊ ◊

The letter of Paul to Philemon raised the fundamental question of ancient Christian attitudes and dealings with slavery. It is clear from the evidence of the New Testament and early Christian literature for at least three centuries more that slavery continued to be practiced by Christians, and explained away in a variety of ways. In the Greco-Roman world, whose economy was heavily based on slavery, it cannot be said that no one questioned the institution of slavery. Legal systems explicitly denied any rights or even legal personhood to slaves, then went on to legislate what slaves and slave-owners could and could not do, as if slaves did have some legal rights. Some philosophers consigned slaves to a nonrational category below free women and children while others affirmed an essential equality in rationality and capacity for virtue of all men (but not women), whether free or slave. Even then, the discrepancy between quasi-egalitarian theory and unequal practice based on differentiation of roles was tolerated without a great deal of conflict, just as it was in relations between men and women.

The freedman philosopher Epictetus discoursed on the nature of freedom by depicting a slave who thinks he will be truly free when manumitted, only to find himself more enslaved than before by the need to cultivate patronage in order to provide for material necessities (*Discourse* 4.1, especially par. 33-40). In these ways slavery was rationalized and freedom characterized as an inner quality regardless of one's social and legal situation. Ancient peoples did not think systemically, and such rationalizations, along with the patronage system that encouraged identification with social superiors rather than with peers, undermined any attempt to analyze an unjust social system.

Paul may have been influenced by these philosophical currents. His expression of indifference toward material want or abundance *(autarkeia)* in Phil 4:11-12 moves in the same direction, as does his assertion that one's legal status at the time of being called to faith makes no difference. He advises all to remain in the state in which they were called, for the freeborn person is Christ's slave and the slave is Christ's freedperson (1 Cor 7:22), even though manumission when possible is not to be discouraged (v. 21). But he quickly turns slavery into a metaphor that applies to everyone (v. 23). Did the reality of baptism make any difference? Did those who were baptized into Christ Jesus, in whom there was no longer Jew or Greek (Gal 3:28), begin to see that the implications led toward social change? The letter to Philemon may give us an early glimpse of just such an intuition.

In the following years the voice of leadership reaffirmed the spiritualization of slavery begun by Paul in 1 Cor 7:23 by applying the principle of Matt 25:40—what is done to another is done to Christ—to the role of slaves. When they serve others, it is really the Lord they are serving (Eph 6:5-8; Col 3:22-25). First Peter 2:18-25 reinforced the approach by making the notion of slaves suffering unjustly the figure of the suffering Christ, a strongly supportive image for slaves who were powerless to protect themselves, but also an enhancement of the spiritual mystique of slavery. In the next generation, we get a hint that slaves may have been taking their brotherly relationship with their owners more seriously than some church leaders liked. Titus 2:9-10 enjoins slaves to be submissive, respectful, and honest. First Timothy 6:1-2 warns slaves not to take too seriously the fact that they and their owners are brothers and sisters, but to serve all the more diligently. Finally, from the other side Ignatius instructs Polycarp not to be arrogant to slaves, but at the same time not to let slaves be arrogant. Returning to the spiritualization approach, he adds that they should, rather, serve all the better in order to have a better freedom from God. He also decrees that slaves should not expect to be set free at community expense, suggesting that such a practice has been established in some places (Ign. *Pol.* 4.3).

Thus we see that the problem was not to be sorted out quickly. The tendency of leadership was not to question, but rather to give a new spiritual rationale for an existing situation, while urging owners against mistreatment (Eph 6:9; Col 4:1). But Philemon should not be interpreted in the light of later household codes and church advice. In this earlier situation, Paul sees the possibility of a new relationship of brotherhood between two men who had been alienated by social structures and by recent actions. That is his hope. That may be as far as the vision went for the moment.

SELECT BIBLIOGRAPHY

WORKS CITED IN THE TEXT
(EXCLUDING COMMENTARIES)

Abrahamsen, Valerie A. 1995. *Women and Worship at Philippi: Diana/Artemis and Other Cults in the Early Christian Era.* Portland, ME: Astarte Shell Press.

Bakirtzis, Charalambos and Helmut Koester, eds. 1998. *Philippi at the Time of Paul and After His Death.* Harrisburg, PA: Trinity Press International.

Barclay, John M. G. 1991. "Paul, Philemon and the Dilemma of Christian Slave-Ownership." *NTS* 37:161-86.

Bartchy, S. Scott. 1992. "Slavery: New Testament." *ABD* 6:65-73.

Basevi, Claudio, and Juan Chapa. 1993. "Philippians 2.6-11: The Rhetorical Function of a Pauline 'Hymn.' " In *Rhetoric and the New Testament: Essays from the 1992 Heidelberg Conference*, edited by Stanley E. Porter and Thomas H. Olbricht, 338-56. JSNTSup 90. Sheffield: *JSOT.*

Bloomquist, L. Gregory. 1993. *The Function of Suffering in Philippians.* JSNTSup 78. Sheffield: JSOT.

Callahan, Allen D. 1995a. "Paul's Epistle to Philemon: Toward an Alternative Argumentum." *HTR* 86:357-76.

———. 1995b. "John Chrysostom on Philemon: A Response to Margaret M. Mitchell." HTR 88:149-56.

Dahl, Nils A. 1995. "Euodia and Syntyche and Paul's Letter to the Philippians." In *The Social World of the First Christians: Essays in Honor of Wayne A. Meeks*, edited by L. Michael White and O. Larry Yarbrough. Minneapolis: Fortress, 3-14.

Fitzgerald, John T. 1996. "Philippians in the Light of Some Ancient Discussions of Friendship." In *Friendship, Flattery, and Frankness of Speech: Studies on Friendship in the New Testament World*, edited by John T. Fitzgerald, 141-60. NovTSup 82. Leiden: E. J. Brill.

Furnish, Victor Paul. 1985. *The Moral Teaching of Paul: Selected Issues.* Rev. ed. Nashville: Abingdon.

Garland, David E. 1985. "The Composition and Unity of Philippians." *NovT* 27:141-73.

Harrill, J. Albert. 1995. *The Manumission of Slaves in Early Christianity.* Hermeneutische Untersuchungen zur Theologie 32. Tübingen: Mohr-Siebeck.

———. 1999. "Using the Roman Jurists to Interpret Philemon: A Response to Peter Lampe." *ZNW* 90:135-38.

Hays, Richard B. 1989. *Echoes of Scripture in the Letters of Paul.* New Haven, CT: Yale University Press.

Hengel, Martin. 1977. *Crucifixion in the Ancient World and the Folly of the Message of the Cross.* Philadelphia: Fortress.

Horsley, G. H. R., and S. R. Llewelyn, eds. 1981–. *New Documents Illustrating Early Christianity.* 8 vols. to date. Sydney: Macquarie University, vols. 1–7. Vol. 8, Sydney: Macquarie University; Grand Rapids, MI: Eerdmans.

Horsley, Richard A., ed. 1997. *Paul and Empire: Religion and Power in Roman Imperial Society.* Valley Forge, PA: Trinity Press International.

Karris, Robert J. 1996. *A Symphony of New Testament Hymns.* Collegeville, MN: Liturgical Press.

Käsemann, Ernst. 1968. "A Critical Analysis of Philippians 2:5-11." *JTC* 5:45-88.

Keller, Marie Noel. 1995. "Choosing What Is Best: Paul, Roman Society and Philippians." Th.D. diss., Lutheran School of Theology.

Kittredge, Cynthia Briggs. 1996. "The Language of Obedience in the Pauline Tradition: Rhetorical Analysis and Historical Reconstruction of the Letters to the Philippians and to the Ephesians." Th.D. diss., Harvard University.

Knox, John. 1959. *Philemon Among the Letters of Paul.* Nashville: Abingdon.

Koperski, Veronica. 1992. "Feminist Concerns and the Authorial Readers in Philippians," *LS* 17:269-92.

———. 1996. *The Knowledge of Christ Jesus My Lord: The High Christology of Philippians 3:7-11. Contributions to Biblical Exegesis and Theology 16.* Kampen: Kok Pharos.

Lampe, Peter. 1985. "Keine 'Sklavenflucht' des Onesimus." *ZNW* 76:135-37.

Lewis, Lloyd L. 1991. "An African American Appraisal of the

Philemon-Paul-Onesimus Triangle," in *Stony the Road We Trod: African American Biblical Interpretation,* edited by Cain Hope Felder, 232-46. Minneapolis: Fortress.

Lüderitz, Gerd. 1994. "What Is the *Politeuma?*" in *Studies in Early Jewish Epigraphy,* edited by Jan Willem Van Heuten and Pieter Willem Van der Horst, 183-225. AGJU. Leiden: E. J. Brill.

Marshall, I. Howard. 1993. "Paul's Ethical Appeal in Philippians." In *Rhetoric and the New Testament: Essays from the 1992 Heidelberg Conference,* edited by Stanley E. Porter and Thomas H. Olbricht, 357-74. JSNTSup 90. Sheffield: *JSOT.*

Martens, John W. 1992. "Ignatius and Onesimus: John Knox Reconsidered." *SecCent* 9:73-86.

Martin, Ralph P. 1983. *Carmen Christi: Philippians 2:5-11 in Recent Interpretation and in the Setting of Early Christian Worship.* Rev. ed. Grand Rapids, MI: Eerdmans.

Martin, Ralph P., and Brian J. Dodd, eds. 1998. *Where Christology Began: Essays on Philippians 2.* Louisville: Westminster John Knox.

Mitchell, Margaret M. 1995. "John Chrysostom on Philemon: A Second Look." *HTR* 88:135-48.

Murphy-O'Connor, Jerome. 1995. *Paul the Letter-Writer: His World, His Options, His Skills.* GNS 41. Collegeville, MN: Michael Glazier, Liturgical Press.

———. 1996. *Paul: A Critical Life.* Oxford: Clarendon.

Nordling, John G. 1991. "Onesimus Fugitivus: A Defense of the Runaway Slave Hypothesis in Philemon." *JSNT* 41:97-119.

Otto, Randall E. 1995. " 'If Possible I May Attain the Resurrection from the Dead' (Philippians 3:11)." *CBQ* 57:324-40.

Palmer, W. D. 1975. " 'To Die Is Gain.' (Phil i 21)." *NovT* 17:203-18.

Peterlin, Davorin. 1995. *Paul's Letter to the Philippians in the Light of Disunity in the Church.* NovTSup 79. Leiden: E. J. Brill.

Peterman, G. W. 1997. *Paul's Gift from Philippi: Conventions of Gift Exchange and Christian Giving.* SNTSMS 92. Cambridge: Cambridge University Press.

Peterson, Norman R. 1985. *Rediscovering Paul: Philemon and the Sociology of Paul's Narrative World.* Philadelphia: Fortress.

Portefaix, Lilian. 1988. *Sisters Rejoice: Paul's Letter to the Philippians and Luke–Acts as Received by First-Century Philippian Women.* ConBNT 20. Stockholm: Almqvist & Wiksell.

Rapske, Brian M. 1991. "The Prisoner Paul in the Eyes of Onesimus." *NTS* 37:187-203.

Reed, Jeffrey T. 1997. *A Discourse Analysis of Philippians: Method and Rhetoric in the Debate over Literary Integrity.* JSNTSup 136. Sheffield: Sheffield Academic Press.

Reumann, John. 1993. "Contributions of the Philippian Community to Paul and to Earliest Christianity." *NTS* 39:438-57.

Sampley, J. Paul. 1980. *Pauline Partnership in Christ: Christian Community and Commitment in Light of Roman Law.* Philadelphia: Fortress.

Snyman, A. H. 1993. "Persuasion in Philippians 4.1-20." In *Rhetoric and the New Testament: Essays from the 1992 Heidelberg Conference,* edited by Stanley E. Porter and Thomas H. Olbricht, 325-37. JSNTSup 90. Sheffield: JSOT.

Stowers, Stanley K. 1986. *Letter Writing in Greco-Roman Antiquity.* Library of Early Christianity. Philadelphia: Westminster.

———. 1991. "Friends and Enemies in the Politics of Heaven: Reading Theology in Philippians." In *Pauline Theology,* edited by Jouette M. Bassler, 105-21. Minneapolis: Fortress.

Watson, D. F. 1988. "A Rhetorical Analysis of Philippians and Its Implications for the Unity Question." *NovT* 30:57-88.

White, L. Michael. 1990. "Morality Between Two Worlds: A Paradigm of Friendship in Philippians." In *Greeks, Romans, and Christians: Essays in Honor of Abraham J. Malherbe,* edited by David L. Balch, Everett Ferguson, and Wayne A. Meeks, 201-15. Minneapolis: Fortress.

Winter, Bruce W. 1994. *Seek the Welfare of the City: Christians As Benefactors and Citizens: First Century Christians in the Greco-Roman World.* Grand Rapids, MI: Eerdmans.

Winter, Sara C. 1987. "Paul's Letter to Philemon." *NTS* 33:1-15.

COMMENTARIES (BOTH CITED AND NOT CITED)

Bartchy, S. Scott. 1992. "Epistle to Philemon." *ABD* 5:305-10. Succinct coverage, using Lampe's theory of flight to a third, mediating party.

Beare, Francis W. 1973. *The Epistle to the Philippians.* Black's New Testament Commentaries. 3rd ed. London: Adam and Charles Black. A classic scholarly commentary useful to those without knowledge of Greek.

Bockmuehl, Mark. 1998. *The Epistle to the Philippians.* Black's New Testament Commentaries. Peabody, MA: Hendrickson. A lucid and solid commentary along traditional lines, with emphasis on theological interpretation.

Bruce, F. F. *Philippians*. 1995. NIBC. Peabody, MA: Hendrickson. A commentary for the general reader based on the NIV translation, which is written by one of the foremost conservative evangelical scholars.

Callahan, Allen D. 1997. *Embassy of Onesimus: The Letter of Paul to Philemon*. The New Testament in Context. Valley Forge, PA: Trinity Press International. A brief, succinct commentary that argues Callahan's thesis at its best.

Fee, Gordon D. 1995. *Paul's Letter to the Philippians*. NICNT. Grand Rapids, MI: Eerdmans. A very comprehensive commentary from an eminent scholar, full of wise perspectives.

Getty, Mary Ann. 1980. *Philippians and Philemon*. New Testament Message 14. Wilmington, DE: Michael Glazier. A readable commentary well suited for pastoral purposes.

Hawthorne, Gerald F. 1983. *Philippians*. WBC 43. Waco, TX: Word. Standard commentary in a respected series, especially good for extended bibliography.

Houlden, J. L. 1970. *Paul's Letters from Prison: Philippians, Colossians, Philemon, and Ephesians*. A classic commentary from a traditional perspective.

Lightfoot, Joseph Barber. 1868. Reprint 1982. *St. Paul's Epistle to the Philippians*. Lynn, MA: Hendrickson. Greek text with extensive notes. A detailed and still surprisingly useful work, with a treasure of cross-references.

———. 1875. *St. Paul's Epistles to the Colossians and to Philemon*. Rev. ed. Lynn, MA: Hendrickson. A classic old commentary, still valuable for its exegetical insights.

Lohse, Eduard. 1971. *Colossians and Philemon*. Translated by William R. Poehlmann and Robert J. Karris. Hermeneia. Philadelphia: Fortress. A solid commentary along traditional lines without benefit of newer theories.

Martin, Ralph P. 1974. *Colossians and Philemon*. NCB. London: Oliphants. Brief but good coverage.

———. 1976. *Philippians*. NCB. London: Oliphants. A commentary for the general reader by one of the foremost scholars on Philippians.

O'Brien, Peter T. 1991. *Commentary on Philippians*. NIGTC. Grand Rapids, MI: Eerdmans. A very careful and complete commentary on the Greek text.

Silva, Moisés. 1988. *Philippians.* Wycliffe Exegetical Commentaries. Chicago: Moody Bible Institute. A conservative evangelical commentary with good technical exegesis based on the Greek text.

Witherington, Ben III. 1994. *Friendship and Finances in Philippi: The Letter of Paul to the Philippians.* The New Testament in Context. Valley Forge, PA: Trinity Press International. A fine commentary in an excellent series, short but very comprehensive.

INDEX